히어로 왕초보 한국어 회화

HERO
KOREAN CONVERSATION

for Beginner

히어로 왕초보 **한국어 회화** English ver.

HERO **KOREAN CONVER**SATION

for Beginner

3rd Edition published	2024.9.1.
1st Edition published	2020.6.30.

written by	the Calling
supervised by	Colin Moore
edited by	Kim Eunkyung
copy-edited by	Lee Jeeyoung
voice actor	Um Hyunjung / Tina Kim

publisher	Cho Kyung-a
published by	LanguageBooks (101-90-85278, 2008.7.10.)
address	208 Bellavista, (390-14, Hapjeong-dong)
	31, Poeun-ro 2na-gil, Mapo-gu, Seoul, Korea
telephone	+82-2-406-0047
fax	+82-2-406-0042
homepage	www.languagebooks.co.kr
e-mail	languagebooks@hanmail.net
mp3 free download	blog.naver.com/languagebook

ISBN	979-11-5635-135-1 (10710)
Price	KRW12,000

© LanguageBooks, 2020

히어로 왕초보 한국어 회화

HERO
KOREAN CONVERSATION
for Beginner

English ver.

Language Books

Preface

As the popularity of K-Pop and Korean dramas
and the charming Korean culture have increased,
the number of Korean learners is increasing.
The easy-to-carry <**Hero Korean Conversation
for Beginner**> for the busy modern life, has
collected only Korean expressions that can be
used in daily life. Even if you are a beginner, kind
Korean will be glad to be your friend.
<**Hero Korean Conversation for Beginner**> will
be a good helper to improve your Korean.

the Calling writer Kim Joenghee

머리말

K-Pop과 한국 드라마 등의 인기 상승 및 매력적인 한국 문화로 한국에 대한 관심이 커져가면서 한국어 학습자도 많아지고 있습니다.

〈**히어로 왕초보 한국어 회화**〉는 바쁜 현대 생활에 어울리는 휴대 간편한 사이즈로, 일상 생활에서 바로 써 먹을 수 있는 한국어 표현만을 모았습니다. 당신이 비록 초보 학습자라도 친절한 한국인 은 기꺼이 당신과 친구가 될 것입니다.

〈**히어로 왕초보 한국어 회화**〉는 당신의 한국어 실력을 발전시킬 좋은 조력자가 될 것입니다.

더 콜링_김정희

About this book

• Speak out without hesitation!

This small-sized book contains conversations for beginners to intermediate Korean learners. We collected the most commonly used expressions in Korea, and it is arranged from introductions to shopping, travel and cases & accidents. Now, don't panic in any Korean emergency situation, find a contextual expression from this book and say with composure.

• Speak out like a native speaker!!

All words are Romanized as closely as possible with pronunciation in the Standard Korean native speaker for beginners. They are included a kind of liaisons(for example, the under consonant sound shifts over to the next syllable).

• Speak out everywhere!!!

It is a pocket-sized, whenever you can find expressions that you want to say something. From now on, <**Hero Korean Conversation for Beginner**> will be a familiar assistant of your Korean language learning.

이 책의 특징

● 막힘없이 쉽게!

왕초보부터 초·중급 수준의 한국어 학습자를 위한 회화 포켓북입니다. 한국 사람들과 바로 통하는 표현을 엄선하여, 인사부터 쇼핑, 여행, 사건&사고까지 세세하게 구성했습니다. 이제 어떠한 한국어 응급상황이 닥치더라도 당황하지 말고, 상황별 표현을 찾아 침착하게 말해 보세요.

● 리얼 발음으로 쉽게!!

왕초보도 쉽게 한국어를 읽을 수 있도록 원어민 표준 발음에 최대한 가깝게 표기했습니다. 단어의 연음까지 반영한 로마자 표기로 이제 자신 있게 원어민 발음을 구사해 보세요.

● 어디서나 쉽게!!!

한 손에 쏙 들어오는 크기로, 언제 어디서나 주머니 속에 휴대하며 필요할 때마다 표현을 찾아 익힐 수 있습니다. 지금부터는 〈히어로 왕초보 한국어 회화〉가 당신의 한국어 학습을 위한 친숙한 조수입니다.

About

Republic of Korea

✓ **Name of Country** Republic of Korea
(대한민국 [대:한민국] dae-han-min-guk)

✓ **Location** Asia (Northeast Asia)

✓ **Capital** Seoul (서울 [서울] seo-ul)

✓ **Official Language** Korean (한국어 [한:구거] han-gu-geo)

✓ **Population** 51.69 million (2024)

✓ **Area** 100,364㎢

✓ **GDP** $1.6 trillion (2024)

✓ **Currency** South Korean Won(KRW)
(원 [원] won)

* **source** www.korea.net, tradingeconomics.com

About Korean Language & Letters
한국어와 한글 han-gu-geo-wa han-geul

Hangeul 한글 han-geul

MP3. C0

Hangeul is the Korean alphabet. This written form of the Korean language was commissioned by King Sejong (1397-1450) during the Joseon Dynasty and made the nation's official script in 1446. Hangeul today is composed of nineteen consonants and twenty-one vowels.

1. **Consonants** 자음 ja-eum

   tip. Consonants in the Korean alphabet may sound differently depending on whether they are the initial or final letter in a syllable. Some consonants only appear in either the initial or final position in a syllable.

10

• 9 plain consonants

letter	letter's name	sample word	meaning
ㄱ	기역 gi-yeok	가구 [가구] ga-gu	furniture
ㄴ	니은 ni-eun	나비 [나비] na-bi	butterfly
ㄷ	디귿 di-geut	다리미 [다리미] da-ri-mi	iron
ㄹ	리을 ri-eul	라디오 [라디오] ra-di-o	radio
ㅁ	미음 mi-eum	마차 [마:차] ma-cha	carriage, wagon
ㅂ	비읍 bi-eup	바지 [바지] ba-ji	trousers, pants
ㅅ	시옷 si-ot	사탕 [사탕] sa-tang	candy
ㅇ	이응 i-eung	아기 [아기] a-gi	baby
ㅈ	지읒 ji-eut	자유 [자유] ja-yu	freedom

• 5 aspirated consonants

letter	letter's name	sample word	meaning
ㅊ	치읓 chi-eut	차표 [차표] cha-pyo	ticket
ㅋ	키읔 ki-euk	카메라 [카메라] ka-me-ra	camera
ㅌ	티읕 ti-eut	타조 [타:조] ta-jo	ostrich
ㅍ	피읖 pi-eup	파도 [파도] pa-do	wave
ㅎ	히읗 hi-eut	하마 [하마] ha-ma	hippopotamus

• 5 tense consonants

letter	letter's name	sample word	meaning
ㄲ	쌍기역 ssang-gi-yeok	까치 [까:치] gga-chi	magpie
ㄸ	쌍디귿 ssang-di-geut	딸기 [딸:기] ddal-gi	strawberry
ㅃ	쌍비읍 ssang-bi-eup	빨래 [빨래] bbal-rae	laundry
ㅆ	쌍시옷 ssang-si-ot	쌍둥이 [쌍둥이] ssang-dung-i	twins
ㅉ	쌍지읒 ssang-ji-eut	짜장면 [짜장면] jja-jang-myeon	black bean sauce noodles

12

tip. Consonants in the Korean alphabet can be combined into 11 consonant clusters, which always appear in the final position in a syllable. They are: ㄳ, ㄵ, ㄶ, ㄺ, ㄻ, ㄼ, ㄽ, ㄾ, ㄿ, ㅀ, and ㅄ.

2. **Vowels** 모음 mo-eum

• **6 simple vowels**

letter	letter's name	sample word	meaning
ㅏ	아 a	바나나 [바나나] ba-na-na	banana
ㅓ	어 eo	어머니 [어머니] eo-meo-ni	mother
ㅗ	오 o	도로 [도ː로] do-ro	road
ㅜ	우 u	구두 [구두] gu-du	shoes
─	으 eu	드레스 [드레스] deu-re-seu	dress
ㅣ	이 i	기린 [기린] gi-rin	giraffe

• 9 compound vowels

letter	letter's name	sample word	meaning
ㅐ	애 ae	냄새 [냄:새] naem-sae	smell
ㅔ	에 e	세제 [세:제] se-je	detergent
ㅘ	와 wa	과일 [과:일] gwa-il	fruit
ㅙ	왜 wae	돼지 [돼:지] dwae-ji	pig
ㅚ	외 oe	외국 [외:국/웨:국] oe-guk/we-guk	foreign country
ㅝ	워 wo	권투 [권:투] gwon-tu	boxing
ㅞ	웨 we	웨이터 [웨이터] we-i-teo	waiter
ㅟ	위 wi	취미 [취:미] chwi-mi	hobby
ㅢ	의 ui	의자 [의자] ui-ja	chair

14

• 6 iotized vowels

letter	letter's name	sample word	meaning
ㅑ	야 ya	야구 [야:구] ya-gu	baseball
ㅕ	여 yeo	여자 [여자] yeo-ja	woman
ㅛ	요 yo	교수 [교:수] gyo-su	professor
ㅠ	유 yu	유리 [유리] yu-ri	glass
ㅒ	얘 yae	얘기 [얘:기] yae-gi	story
ㅖ	예 ye	예약 [예:약] ye-yak	reservation

Unit 4 Banks & Post Offices

Chapter 4 For My Trip

Unit 1 Departure

Unit 2 At the Airport

Chapter 5 Tough Times

Chapter 1

Communication Basics

First Meetings

\# Hello. / Hi.

안녕(하세요).

an-nyeoung(-ha-se-yo)

\# How do you do?

처음 뵙겠습니다.

cheo-eum boep-gget-sseum-ni-da

\# I don't think we've met. I'm Ji-na Kim.

초면인 것 같네요. 저는 김지나입니다.

cho-myeo-nin geot gat-ne-yo. jeo-neun gim-ji-na-im-ni-da

\# Nice to meet you.

만나서 반가워(요).

man-na-seo ban-ga-wo(-yo)

\# Nice to meet you too.

저도 반갑습니다.

jeo-do ban-gap-sseum-ni-da

I'm honored to meet you.

만나 뵙게 되어 영광입니다.

man-na boep-gge doe-eo yeong-gwang-im-ni-da

I've heard so much about you.

말씀 많이 들었어요.

mal-sseum ma-ni deu-reo-sseo-yo

Seong-hee, have you met Jun-ho Kim?

성희 씨, 김준호 씨 아세요?

seong-hi ssi, gim-jun-ho ssi a-se-yo?

My name is Jin-su Park. I'm a friend of Jun-ho Kim.

박진수라고 합니다. 김준호의 친구입니다.

bak-jjin-su-ra-go ham-ni-da. gim-jun-ho-e chin-gu-im-ni-da

Have we ever met before?

전에 우리 만난 적 있나요?

jeo-ne u-ri man-nan jeok in-na-yo?

May I have your business card?

명함 있으세요?

myeong-ham i-sseu se-yo?

Here's my card.

제 명함입니다.

je myeong-ha-mim-ni-da

Situational Greetings

Good morning.

좋은 아침이에요.

jo-eun a-chi-mi-e-yo

잘 잤어(요)?

jal ja-sseo(-yo)?

안녕히 주무셨어요?

an-nyeong-hi ju-mu-syeo-sseo-yo?

Good night.

잘 자(요).

jal ja(-yo)

안녕히 주무세요.

an-nyeong-hi ju-mu-se-yo

Thanks for the food.

잘 먹겠습니다.

jal meok-gget-sseum-ni-da

I enjoyed it.

잘 먹었습니다.

jal meo-geot-sseum-ni-da

Giving Regards

Long time no see.

오랜만입니다.

o-raen-ma-nim-ni-da

I haven't seen you for a long time.

오랫동안 뵙지 못했네요.

o-raet-ddong-an boep-jji mo-taet-ne-yo

I beg your pardon for my long silence.

오랫동안 연락하지 못해 죄송합니다.

o-raet-ddong-an yeol-ra-ka-ji mo-tae joe-song-ham-ni-da

Did you have a meal?

식사했어(요)?

sik-ssa-hae-sseo(-yo)?

How are you? / How are you doing?

어떻게 지내(요)?

eo-ddeo-ke ji-nae(-yo)?

잘 지내(요)?

jal ji-nae(-yo)?

How have you been doing?

어떻게 지내셨어요?

eo-ddeo-ke ji-nae-syeo-sseo-yo?

How's about your parents?

부모님은 모두 잘 계세요?

bu-mo-ni-meun mo-du jal gye-se-yo?

How's about your family?

가족들은 모두 잘 지내(요)?

ga-jok-ddeu-reun mo-du jal ji-nae(-yo)?

What's going on?

별일 없어(요)?

byeol-ril eop-sseo(-yo)?

How was your weekend?

주말 어땠어(요)?

ju-mal eo-ddae-sseo(-yo)?

You haven't changed a bit.

하나도 안 변했네(요).

ha-na-do an byeon-haen-ne(-yo)

I haven't seen much of you lately.

요즘 보기 힘드네(요).

yo-jeum bo-gi him-deu-ne(-yo)

What's the matter?

어디 안 좋아(요)?

eo-di an jo-a(-yo)?

무슨 일이에요?

mu-seun i-ri-e-yo?

Pretty good. / I'm doing well.

잘 지내(요).

jal ji-nae(-yo)

Not too bad. / So so.

그럭저럭(요).

geu-reok-jjeo-reok(-yo)

그럭저럭 지내(요).

geu-reok-jjeo-reok ji-nae(-yo)

Same as usual.

여전해(요).

yeo-jeon-hae(-yo)

Nothing special.

별일 없어(요).

byeol-ril eop-sseo(-yo)

특별한 일 없어(요).

teuk-bbyeol-han il eop-sseo(-yo)

I'm just in a bad mood.

그냥 기분이 안 좋아(요).

geu-nyang gi-bu-ni an jo-a(-yo)

Say hello to your parents for me.

제 대신 부모님께 안부 전해 주세요.

je dae-sin bu-mo-nim-gge an-bu jeon-hae ju-se-yo

Saying Good-bye

Good-bye.

잘 가(요). / 안녕(히 가세요).

jal ga(-yo) / an-nyeong(-hi ga-se-yo)

See you tomorrow.

내일 만나(요). / 내일 봐요.

nae-il man-na(-yo) / nae-il bwae-yo

See you again.

또 만나(요).

ddo man-na(-yo)

See you later.

이따가 만나(요).

i-dda-ga man-na(-yo)

See you there, then.

그럼, 거기에서 만나(요).

geu reom, geo-gi-e-seo man-na(-yo)

Let's get together soon.

조만간에 만나(요).

jo-man-ga-ne man-na(-yo)

Have a nice day.

좋은 날 되세요.

jo-eun nal doe-se-yo

Have a nice weekend.

주말 잘 보내(요).

ju-mal jal bo-nae(-yo)

Take care.

조심히 가세요.

jo-sim-hi ga-se-yo

살펴 가세요.

sal-pyeo ga-se-yo

I'll see myself out.
나오지 마(세요).

na-o-ji ma(-se-yo)

Keep in touch.
연락하고 지내자.

yeol-ra-ka-go ji-nae-ja

Enjoy your trip!
즐거운 여행 되세요!

jeul-geo-un yeo-haeng doe-se-yo!

Have fun. / Have a good day.
다녀오세요.

da-nyeo-o-se-yo

I'm home. / I'm back.
다녀왔습니다.

da-nyeo-wat-sseum-ni-da

Welcoming

Welcome to Seoul.

서울에 오신 것을 환영합니다.

seo-u-re o-sin geo-seul hwa-nyeong-ham-ni-da

Welcome to my home.

저희 집에 오신 것을 환영합니다.

jeo-hi ji-be o-sin geo-seul hwa-nyeong-ham-ni-da

I hope you'll like it here.

이곳이 마음에 들었으면 좋겠어(요).

i-go-si ma-eu-me deu-reo-sseu-myeon jo-ke-sseo(-yo)

Welcome. / Come on in.

어서 오세요.

eo-seo o-se-yo

Come in.

들어오세요.

deu-reo-o-se-yo

Getting Attention

Excuse me.

실례합니다.

sil-rye-ham-ni-da

Can I get by, please?

좀 비켜 주시겠어요?

jom bi-kyeo ju-si-ge-sseo-yo?

Hello!

여보세요!

yeo-bo-se-yo!

Ma'am!

아주머니!

a-ju-meo-ni!

Sir!

아저씨!

a-jeo-ssi!

Hey! / Excuse me!

여기요!

yeo-gi-yo!

저기요!

jeo-gi-yo!

Wanting to Talk

I have something to tell you.

할 말이 있는데(요).

hal ma-ri in-neun-de(-yo)

Can I talk to you for a minute?

이야기 좀 해도 될까(요)?

i-ya-gi jom hae-do doel-gga(-yo)?

얘기 좀 해도 될까(요)?

yae-gi jom hae-do doel-gga(-yo)?

May I interrupt you?

말씀 중에 죄송합니다.

mal-sseum jung-e joe-song-ham-ni-da

끼어들어서 미안합니다.

ggi-eo-deu-reo-seo mi-an-ham-ni-da

Let me tell you something.

제 말 좀 들어 봐요.

je mal jom deu-reo bwa-yo

내 말 좀 들어 봐(요).

nae mal jom deu-reo bwa(-yo)

Guess what? / You know what?

있잖아(요).

it-jja-na(-yo)

Getting Information

\# May I have your name? / What's your name?

성함이 어떻게 되세요?

seong-ha-mi eo-ddeo-ke doe-se-yo?

이름이 뭐예요?

i-reu-mi mwo-ye-yo?

\# What do you do for living?

무슨 일 하세요?

mu-seun il ha-se-yo?

직업이 뭐예요?

ji-geo-bi mwo-ye-yo?

\# What's your nationality?

어느 나라 사람이에요?

eo-neu na-ra sa-ra-mi-e-yo?

\# Where are you from?

어디에서 왔어(요)?

eo-di-e-seo wa-sseo(-yo)?

How many languages do you speak?

몇 개 국어를 하세요?

meot gae gu-geo-reul ha-se-yo?

Giving Information

I'm from Korea.

한국에서 왔어(요).

han-gu-ge-seo wa-sseo(-yo)

I'm Korean.

한국 사람입니다.

han-guk sa-ra-mim-ni-da

I work for AB company.

저는 AB회사에 다닙니다.

jeo-neun e-i-bi-hoe-sa-e da-nim-ni-da

I work at a bank.

저는 은행에서 일합니다.

jeo-neun eun-haeng-e-seo il-ham-ni-da

I am a senior at Han-guk University.

저는 한국대학 4학년입니다.

jeo-neun han-guk-ddae-hak sa-hang-nyeo-nim-ni-da

I'm single.

미혼이에요.

mi-ho-ni-e-yo

I'm married.

결혼했어요.

gyeol-hon-hae-sseo-yo

Introducing Oneself

Let me introduce myself.

제 소개를 할게요.

je so-gae-reul hal-gge-yo

내 소개를 할게(요).

nae so-gae-reul hal-gge(-yo)

May I introduce myself?

저를 소개해도 될까요?

jeo-reul so-gae-hae-do doel-gga-yo?

Hello, I'm Ji-na Kim.

안녕하세요, 김지나라고 합니다.

an-nyeong-ha-se-yo, gim-ji-na-ra-go ham-ni-da

Just call me Ji-na.

그냥 지나라고 불러 주세요.

geu-nyang ji-na-ra-go bul-reo ju-se-yo

Hello, I'm Ji-na Kim, a friend of Ji-mi's.

안녕하세요, 저는 지미의 친구 김지나입니다.

an-nyeong-ha-se-yo, jeo-neun ji-mi-e chin-gu
gim-ji-na-im-ni-da

Gratitude

\# Thank you. / Thanks.

고맙습니다.

go-map-sseum-ni-da

고마워(요).

go-ma-wo(-yo)

\# Thank you very much.

매우 감사합니다.

mae-u gam-sa-ham-ni-da

매우 고마워(요).

mae-u go-ma-wo(-yo)

\# I don't know how to thank you enough.

뭐라고 감사해야 할지 모르겠네(요).

mwo-ra-go gam-sa-hae-ya hal-jji mo-reu-gen-ne(-yo)

Thank you anyway.

어찌됐든 고맙습니다.

eo-jji-dwaet-ddeun go-map-sseum-ni-da

아무튼 고마워(요).

a-mu-teun go-ma-wo(-yo)

Thank you for everything.

여러 가지로 감사합니다.

yeo-reo ga-ji-ro gam-sa-ham-ni-da

여러 가지로 고마워(요).

yeo-reo ga-ji-ro go-ma-wo(-yo)

I'd like to express my thanks.

감사의 뜻을 전합니다.

gam-sa-e ddeu-seul jeon-ham-ni-da

You're a life saver.

당신은 제 생명의 은인이에요.

dang-si-neun je saeng-myeong-e eu-ni-ni-e-yo

I'll never forget what you have done for me.

제 평생 당신의 은혜를 잊지 못할 거예요.

je pyeong-saeng dang-si-ne eun-hye-reul it-jji mo-tal
ggeo-ye-yo

Thank you for all the trouble you've gone to.

마음 써 주셔서 감사드립니다.

ma-eum sseo ju-syeo seo gam-sa-deu-rim-ni-da

Thank you very much for your help.

도와주셔서 대단히 감사드립니다.

do-wa-ju-syeo-seo dae-dan-hi gam-sa-deu-rim-ni-da

I appreciate the invitation.

초대에 감사드립니다.

cho-dae-e gam-sa-deu-rim-ni-da

I appreciate your concern.

당신의 관심에 감사합니다.

dang-si-ne gwan-si-me gam-sa-ham-ni-da

Thank you for your kindness.

당신의 친절에 감사합니다.

dang-si-ne chin-jeo-re gam-sa-ham-ni-da

Thank you for giving me a chance.

제게 기회를 주셔서 감사합니다.

je-ge gi-hoe-reul ju-syeo-seo gam-sa-ham-ni-da

Thank you for giving me directions.

길을 안내해 주셔서 감사합니다.

gi-reul an-nae-hae ju-syeo-seo gam-sa-ham-ni-da

Thank you for waiting.

기다려 주셔서 감사합니다.

gi-da-ryeo ju-syeo-seo gam-sa-ham-ni-da

I appreciate your consideration.

배려해 주셔서 감사합니다.

bae-ryeo-hae ju-syeo-seo gam-sa-ham-ni-da

Responding to Gratitude

You're welcome.

천만에(요).

cheon-ma-ne(-yo)

Don't mention it.

별말씀을(요).

byeol-mal-sseu-meul(-yo)

My pleasure.

뭘(요).

mwol(-yo)

I'm honored by your words.

과찬의 말씀이십니다.

gwa-cha-ne mal-sseu-mi-sim-ni-da

I should be the one to thank you.

오히려 제가 감사해야죠.

o-hi-ryeo je-ga gam-sa-hae-ya-jyo

No big deal.

뭐 대단한 일도 아닌데(요).

mwo dae-dàn-han il-do a-nin-de(-yo)

It was my honor to helped you.

당신을 도울 수 있어서 제가 영광입니다.

dang-si-neul do-ul ssu i-sseo-seo je-ga
yeong-gwang-im-ni-da

Apologies

I'm sorry.

미안합니다.

mi-an-ham-ni-da

미안해(요).

mi-an-hae(-yo)

죄송합니다.

joe-song-ham-ni-da

I apologize to you.

사과드립니다.

sa-gwa-deu-rim-ni-da

I'm sorry about that.

그것에 대해 미안합니다.

geu-geo-se dae-hae mi-an-ham-ni-da

I'm sorry to disturb you.

폐를 끼쳐서 죄송합니다.

pye-reul ggi-cheo-seo joe-song-ham-ni-da

Excuse me for being late.

늦어서 죄송합니다.

neu-jeo-seo joe-song-ham-ni-da

I'm sorry to have kept you waiting so long.

오래 기다리게 해서 미안합니다.

o-rae gi-da-ri-ge hae-seo mi-an-ham-ni-da

It won't happen again.

다시는 이런 일이 일어나지 않을 것입니다.

da-si-neun i-reon i-ri i-reo-na-ji a-neul ggeo-sim-ni-da

I'm sorry if it offended you.

기분 나빴다면 미안해(요).

gi-bun na-bbat-dda-myeon mi-an-hae(-yo)

I'd like to say I'm sorry.

미안하다는 말을 하고 싶어(요).

mi-an-ha-da-neun ma-reul ha-go si-peo(-yo)

I don't know what to apologize.

뭐라고 사과해야 할지 모르겠어(요).

mwo-ra-go sa-gwa-hae-ya hal-jji mo-reu-ge-sseo(-yo)

Please accept my apology.
부디 제 사과를 받아 주세요.
bu-di je sa-gwa-reul ba-da ju-se-yo

I owe you an apology for my mistake.
제 실수에 대해 사과드립니다.
je sil-ssu-e dae-hae sa-gwa-deu-rim-ni-da

Making a Mistake

I'm sorry, I couldn't help it.
미안해요, 저도 어쩔 수 없어요.
mi-an-hae-yo, jeo-do eo-jjeol ssu eop-sseo-yo

I'm sorry, I forgot it.
미안해(요), 깜박 잊었어(요).
mi-an-hae(-yo), ggam-bak i-jeo-sseo(-yo)

I'm sorry, I didn't do it on purpose.
미안해(요), 고의가 아니었어(요).
mi-an-hae(-yo), go-i-ga a-ni-eo-sseo(-yo)

Give me a chance to make it up to you.

만회할 기회를 주세요.

man-hoe-hal gi-hoe-reul ju-se-yo

I can only blame myself.

그저 제 탓입니다.

geu-jeo je ta-sim-ni-da

Sorry that I blew it.

제가 망쳐서 죄송합니다.

je-ga mang-cheo-seo joe-song-ham-ni-da

Answering Apologies

That's okay. / It's okay.

괜찮아(요).

gwaen-cha-na(-yo)

It is I who must apologize.

저야말로 사과를 드려야죠.

jeo-ya-mal-ro sa-gwa-reul deu-ryeo-ya-jyo

You're forgiven.

용서할게(요).

yong-seo-hal-gge(-yo)

Let's forgive and forget.

서로 용서하고 잊어버리자.

seo-ro yong-seo-ha-go i-jeo-beo-ri-ja

Don't worry about that.

걱정하지 마(세요).

geok-jjeong-ha-ji ma(-se-yo)

There's nothing to forgive.

미안해할 거 없어(요).

mi-an-hae-hal ggeo eop-sseo(-yo)

Poor Understanding

\# Sorry, but I can't hear you.

미안해(요), 못 들었어(요).

mi-an-hae(-yo), mot deu-reo-sseo(-yo)

\# You're speaking too quickly for me.

말이 너무 빨라(요).

ma-ri neo-mu bbal-ra(-yo)

\# I don't quite get you.

잘 모르겠어(요).

jal mo-reu-ge-sseo(-yo)

\# I didn't catch what you said.

당신의 말을 이해할 수 없어요.

dang-si-ne ma-reul i-hae-hal ssu eop-sseo-yo

\# What does that mean?

무슨 뜻이죠?

mu-seun ddeu-si-jyo?

Say what?

뭐라고(요)?

mwo-ra-go(-yo)?

Asking to Be Excused

Excuse me, may I get through?

실례지만, 좀 비켜 주세요.

sil-rye-ji-man, jom bi-kyeo ju-se-yo

Excuse me for just a moment, I'll be back soon.

잠시 실례해요, 곧 돌아올게요.

jam-si sil-rye-hae-yo, got do-ra-ol-gge-yo

Something happened, I've got to go.

일이 있어서, 가야겠어(요).

i-ri i-sseo-seo, ga-ya-ge-sseo(-yo)

Can you keep an eye on my bag? Nature's calling.

화장실에 가려는데, 제 가방 좀 봐 줄 수 있어요?

hwa-jang-si-re ga-ryeo-neun-de, je ga-bang jom bwa jul ssu i-sseo-yo?

Excuse me, but I think you're sitting in my seat.

실례지만, 제 자리에 앉아 계신 것 같은데요.

sil-rye-ji-man, je ja-ri-e an-ja gye-sin geot ga-teun-de-yo

Positive Replies

Sure. / Of course.

당연히 되죠.

dang-yeon-hi doe-jyo

당연하죠.

dang-yeon-ha-jyo

당연하지.

dang-yeon-ha-ji

물론이죠.

mul-ro-ni-jyo

I got it. / Yes, sir.

알겠어(요).

al-ge-sseo(-yo)

Yes, I'd be happy to.

그래(요).

geu-rae(-yo)

All right.

좋아(요).

jo-a(-yo)

You're right.

맞아(요).

ma-ja(-yo)

I'd be glad to.

기꺼이 할게(요).

gi-ggeo-i hal-gge(-yo)

Yes, I'd be happy to.

이렇게 할 수 있어 기뻐(요).

i-reo-ke hal ssu i-sseo gi-bbeo(-yo)

Negative Replies

\# I'll never get it right.

전혀 모르겠는네(요).

jeon-hyeo mo-reu-gen-neun-de(-yo)

\# I have no idea.

방법이 없어(요).

bang-beo-bi eop-sseo(-yo)

\# I'll never figure it out.

해결할 수 없어(요).

hae-gyeol-hal ssu eop-sseo(-yo)

\# Not at all.

아무것도 아니에요.

a-mu-geot-ddo a-ni-e-yo

\# Not yet.

아직이요.

a-ji-gi-yo

아직.

a-jik

Of course not.

물론 아니죠.

mul-ron a-ni-jyo

당연히 아니에요.

dang-yeon-hi a-ni-e-yo

Polite Refusals

I'm afraid not.

유감이지만, 안 될 거 같은데(요).

yu-ga-mi-ji-man, an doel ggeo ga-teun-de(-yo)

I don't think so.

그렇게 생각하지 않는데(요).

geu-reo-ke saeng-ga-ka-ji an-neun-de(-yo)

I don't think I can make it.

제가 할 수 없을 것 같아요.

je-ga hal ssu eop-sseul ggeot ga-ta-yo

I can't make it.

저도 어쩔 도리가 없어요.

jeo-do eo-jjeol do-ri-ga eop-sseo-yo

Sorry, I can't right now.

미안해(요), 지금은 안 돼(요).

mi-an-hae(-yo), ji-geu-meun an dwae(-yo)

It's not the best time.

최선의 시간이 아닙니다.

choe-seo-ne si-ga-ni a-nim-ni-da

Other Replies

It's possible.

이것은 가능해(요).

i-geo-seun ga-neung-hae(-yo)

Maybe. / Perhaps.

아마도(요).

a-ma-do(-yo)

Well.

글쎄(요).

geul-sse(-yo)

It depends.

경우에 따라 달라(요).

gyeong-u-e dda-ra dal-ra(-yo)

그것에 달려 있어(요).

geu-geo-se dal-ryeo i-sseo(-yo)

I'll give it some thought.

좀 고려해 볼게(요).

jom go-ryeo-hae bol-gge(-yo)

It's hard to believe.

믿기 어려운데(요).

mit-ggi eo-ryeo-un-de(-yo)

I can't believe it.

믿을 수 없어(요).

mi-deul ssu eop-sseo(-yo)

No kidding.

농담하지 마(세요).

nong-dam-ha-ji ma(-se-yo)

상난치지 마(세요).

jang-nan-chi-ji ma(-se-yo)

That's a lame joke.

썰렁해(요).

sseol-reong-hae(-yo)

I don't feel like it.

그럴 기분이 아니에요.

geu-reol gi-bu-ni a-ni-e-yo

Can you understand what I said?

내 말 이해했어(요)?

nae mal i-hae-hae-sseo(-yo)?

No comment.

드릴 말씀이 없습니다.

deu-ril mal-sseu-mi eop-sseum-ni-da

Agreeing

Right.

맞아(요).

ma-ja(-yo)

That's it.

바로 그거예요.

ba-ro geu-geo-ye-yo

So do I.

저도요.

jeo-do-yo

I think so.

저도 이렇게 생각해요.

jeo-do i-reo-ke saeng-ga-kae-yo

저도 그렇게 생각해요.

jeo-do geu-reo-ke saeng-ga-kae-yo

That's a good idea.

좋은 생각이에요.

jo-eun saeng-ga-gi-e-yo

There is no objection on my part.

이견이 없는데(요).

i-gyeo-ni eom-neun-de(-yo)

I agree.

동의합니다.

dong-i-ham-ni-da

찬성합니다.

chan-seong-ham-ni-da

찬성해(요).

chan-seong-hae(-yo)

Yes, indeed.

그렇고말고(요).

geu-reo-ko-mal-go(-yo)

Absolutely.

두말하면 잔소리(죠).

du-mal-ha-myeon jan-so-ri(-jyo)

You're right on the money.

옳으신 말씀입니다.

o-reu-sin mal-sseu-mim-ni-da

I totally agree with you.

무조건 찬성합니다.

mu-jo-ggeon chan-seong-ham-ni-da

전부 찬성해(요).

jeon-bu chan-seong-hae(-yo)

It's unaimous then.

만장일치입니다.

man-jang-il-chi-im-ni-da

Disagreeing

Is that so?

그래(요)?

geu-rae(-yo)?

I'm not sure.

잘 모르겠어(요).

jal mo-reu-ge-sseo(-yo)

You don't say.

그럴리가(요).

geu-reol-ri-ga(-yo)

That might be right.

그럴지도 모르죠.

geu-reol-jji-do mo-reu-jyo

That's not always the case.

꼭 그런 건 아니에요.

ggok geu-reon geon a-ni-e-yo

That's not always true.

꼭 옳은 건 아니에요.

ggok o-reun geon a-ni-e-yo

I disagree.

전 반대예요.

jeon ban-dae-ye-yo

I can't support your opinion.

당신의 의견을 지지하지 않아요.

dang-si-ne ui-gyeo-neul ji-ji-ha-ji a-na-yo

I disagree with you.

당신의 생각에 동의하지 않아요.

dang-si-ne saeng-ga-ge dong-i-ha-ji a-na-yo

I'm opposed to that idea.

그 계획에 반대해(요).

geu gye-hoe-ge ban-dae-hae(-yo)

Are you sure about that?

그것에 대해 확신해(요)?

geu-geo-se dae-hae hwak-ssin-hae(-yo)?

Warnings

Watch out.

조심해(요).

jo-sim-hae(-yo)

Watch out for the cars.

차 조심해(요).

cha jo-sim-hae(-yo)

Watch your tongue.

말할 때 좀 주의해(요).

mal-hal ddae jom ju-i-hae(-yo)

Be quiet.

좀 조용히 해(요).

jom jo-yong-hi hae(-yo)

Don't ask for trouble.

쓸데없는 짓 하지 마(세요).

sseul-dde-eom-neun jit ha-ji ma(-se-yo)

Don't do that.

그렇게 하지 마(세요).

geu-reo-ke ha-ji ma(-se-yo)

Don't tell anyone.

아무한테도 말하면 안 돼(요).

a-mu-han-te-do mal-ha-myeon an dwae(-yo)

Don't try to flatter me.

비행기 태우지 마(세요).

bi-haeng-gi tae-u-ji ma(-se-yo)

Don't be rude.

무례하게 굴지 마(세요).

mu-rye-ha-ge gul-ji ma(-se-yo)

Don't touch me.

날 건들지 마(세요).

nal geon-deul-ji ma(-se-yo)

Stop bugging me.

날 귀찮게 하지 마(세요).

nal gwi-chan-ke ha-ji ma(-se-yo)

Don't hit my nerve.

내 성질 건드리지 마(세요).

nae seong-jil geon-deu-ri-ji ma(-se-yo)

Don't mind me.

상관하지 마(세요).

sang-gwan-ha-ji ma(-se-yo)

Don't try to get out of it.

오리발 내밀지 마(세요).

o-ri-bal nae-mil-ji ma(-se-yo)

Stop badgering him.

그를 괴롭히지 마(세요).

geu-reul goe-ro-pi-ji ma(-se-yo)

Consider your surroundings.

분위기 파악 좀 해(요).

bun-wi-gi pa-ak jom hae(-yo)

Advising

Remember this.

기억해(요).

gi-eo-kae(-yo)

명심해(요).

myeong-sim-hae(-yo)

Do your best.

최선을 다해라.

choe-seo-neul da-hae-ra

Shame on you.

부끄러운 줄 알아라.

bu-ggeu-reo-un jul a-ra-ra

Pay no attention.

마음에 담아두지 마(세요).

ma-eu-me da-ma-du-ji ma(-se-yo)

You shouldn't act on your impules.

충동적으로 하지 마(세요).

chung-dong-jeo-geu-ro ha-ji ma(-se-yo)

You can say what you want to say.

하고 싶은 말 있으면 다 해라.

ha-go si-peun mal i-sseu-myeon da hae-ra

Get real.

꿈꾸지 마(세요).

ggum-ggu-ji ma(-se-yo)

꿈 깨(요).

ggum ggae(-yo)

You should face the problem.

문제에 맞서라.

mun-je-e mat-sseo-ra

Keep up the good work.

계속 노력해라.

gye-sok no-ryeo-kae-ra

Don't get your hopes up.

너무 기대하지 마(세요).

neo-mu gi-dae-ha-ji ma(-se-yo)

Would you behave yourself?

좀 얌전히 있을래(요)?

jom yam-jeon-hi i-sseul-rae(-yo)?

Brace yourself.

마음의 준비를 잘해라.

ma-eu-me jun-bi-reul jal-hae-ra

Paying Compliments

Great!

대단해(요)!

dae-dan-hae(-yo)!

훌륭해(요)!

hul-ryung-hae(-yo)!

끝내주네(요)!

ggeun-nae-ju-ne(-yo)!

That's terrific! / That's awesome!

정말 멋져(요)!

jeong-mal meot-jjeo(-yo)!

정말 굉장해(요)!

jeong-mal goeng-jang-hae(-yo)!

Good job!

잘했어(요)!

jal-hae-sseo(-yo)!

You're a man[woman] ahead of your time!

넌 시대를 앞선 사람이야!

neon si-dae-reul ap-sseon sa-ra-mi-ya!

You're a walking encyclopedia!

정말 못하는 게 없구나!

jeong-mal mo-ta-neun ge eop-ggu-na!

Encouraging Someone

Come on!

힘내(요)!

him-nae(-yo)!

Cheer up!

기운 내(요)!

gi-un nae(-yo)!

Go for it!

파이팅!

pa-i-ting!

You can do it!

넌 할 수 있어(요)!

neon hal ssu i-sseo(-yo)!

Good luck!

행운을 빌어(요)!

haeng-u-neul bi-reo(-yo)!

Don't give up.

포기하지 마(세요).

po-gi-ha-ji ma(-se-yo)

I'm on your side.

난 네 편이야.

nan ne pyeo-ni-ya

Asking a Favor

Can I ask you a favor?

일 좀 부탁해도 될까(요)?

il jom bu-ta-kae-do doel-gga(-yo)?

Could you help me?

도와줄 수 있어(요)?

do-wa-jul ssu i-sseo(-yo)?

Would you mind opening the window?

창문 좀 열어 줄래(요)?

chang-mun jom yeo-reo jul-rae(-yo)?

Would you like to join me?

함께 갈래(요)?

ham-gge gal-rae(-yo)?

Would you mind bring me a drink?

마실 것 좀 주실래요?

ma-sil ggeot jom ju-sil-rae-yo?

Hurrying Someone

Hurry up.

어서.

eo-seo

서둘러(요).

seo-dul-reo(-yo)

We have to hurry.

우리는 서둘러야 해(요).

u-ri-neun seo-dul-reo-ya hae(-yo)

Let's make it a rush.

서두르자.

seo-du-reu-ja

I'm in a hurry.

제가 좀 급해서요.

je-ga jom geu-pae-seo-yo

Step on it.

좀 더 서둘러 주세요.

jom deo seo-dul-reo ju-se-yo

Quickly, quickly!

빨리, 빨리!

bbal-ri, bbal-ri!

There's no time to lose.

지체할 시간이 없어(요).

ji-che-hal si-ga-ni eop-sseo(-yo)

Guessing

It figures.

그럴 줄 알았어(요).

geu-reol jjul a-ra-sseo(-yo)

You guessed right.

네가 맞았어(요).

ne-ga ma-ja-sseo(-yo)

The results met our expectations.

결과는 우리가 예상한 것과 같아(요).

gyeol-gwa-neun u-ri-ga ye-sang-han geot-ggwa ga-ta(-yo)

Just a wild guess.

그냥 내 멋대로 추측했어(요).

geu-nyang nae meot-ddae-ro chu-cheu-kae-sseo(-yo)

The chances are slim.

가능성은 적어(요).

ga-neung-sseong-eun jeo-geo(-yo)

I had no idea that you were coming.

네가 올 줄 생각도 못했어(요).

ne-ga ol jjul saeng-gak-ddo mo-tae-sseo(-yo)

That's a whole new ball game.

그 일은 의외예요.

geu i-reun ui-oe-ye-yo

Sympathizing

I'm very sorry.

너무 아쉬워(요).

neo-mu a-swi-wo(-yo)

I'm really sorry to hear that.

유감이네(요).

yu-ga-mi-ne(-yo)

Don't lose heart.

너무 실망하지 마(세요).

neo-mu sil-mang-ha-ji ma(-se-yo)

What bad luck!

운이 안 좋았어(요)!

u-ni an jo-a-sseo(-yo)!

That's too bad!

그거 너무 안됐군(요)!

geu-geo neo-mu an-dwaet-ggun(-yo)!

What a pity!

어머, 가엾어라!

eo-meo, ga-yeop-sseo-ra!

Blaming Someone

Silly!

바보!

ba-bo!

You're so stupid!

넌 정말 어리석어!

neon jeong-mal eo-ri-seo-geo!

You're insane.

미쳤구나.

mi-cheot-ggu-na

Have you lost your mind?

생각이 없어(요)?

saeng-ga-gi eop-sseo(-yo)?

정신 나갔어(요)?

jeong-sin na-ga-sseo(-yo)?

What impudence!

뻔뻔하구나!

bbeon-bbeon-ha-gu-na!

철면피구나!

cheol-myeon-pi-gu-na!

염치가 없구나!

yeom-chi-ga eop-ggu-na!

What a shame!

부끄러운 줄 모르는구나!

bu-ggeu-reo-un jul mo-reu-neun-gu-na!

You're disgusting.

정말 구역질 나(요).

jeong-mal gu-yeok-jjil na(-yo)

You're so childish.

정말 유치해(요).

jeong-mal yu-chi-hae(-yo)

Grow up.

철 좀 들어라.

cheol jom deu-reo-ra

You're really something.

정말 너란 건.

jeong-mal neo-ran geon

Why are your acting this way?

어떻게 이럴 수 있어(요)?

eo-ddeo-ke i-reol ssu i-sseo(-yo)?

How dare you talk to me like that!

어찌 감히 나한테 그렇게 말할 수 있어(요)!

eo-jji gam-hi na-han-te geu-reo-ke mal-hal ssu i-sseo(-yo)!

Making a Call

\# Is Se-jin there?

세진이 있어(요)?

se-ji-ni i-sseo(-yo)?

\# Hello, this is Seung-jun. Is Hyun-su there?

여보세요, 승준인데(요). 현수 있어(요)?

yeo-bo-se-yo, seung-ju-nin-de(-yo). hyeon-su i-sseo(-yo)?

\# Could I speak to Ji-yun?

지윤이하고 통화하고 싶은데(요).

ji-yu-ni-ha-go tong-hwa-ha-go si-peun-de(-yo)

\# Can you talk right now?

지금 통화하기 괜찮아(요)?

ji-geum tong-hwa-ha-gi gwaen-cha-na(-yo)?

I'm sorry for calling so late.

이렇게 늦었는데 전화드려서 정말
죄송합니다.

i-reo-ke neu-jeot-neun-de jeon-hwa-deu-ryeo-seo jeonq-mal
joe-song-ham-ni-da

I'm just returning your call.

전화하셨다고 해서 전화드렸습니다.

jeon-hwa-ha-syeot-dda-go hae-seo
jeon-hwa-deu-ryeot-sseum-ni-da

Receiving a Call

Excuse me, who's calling please?

실례지만, 누구세요?

sil-rye-ji-man, nu-gu-se-yo?

May I ask what this is about?

무슨 일이세요?

mu-seun i-ri-se-yo?

Is this an emergency?

급한 용무 있어(요)?

geu-pan yong-mu i-sseo(-yo)?

Who would you like to speak to?

어느 분 찾으세요?

eo-neu bun cha-jeu-se-yo?

Is he expecting your call?

그를 바꿔 드릴까요?

geu-reul ba-ggwo deu-ril-gga-yo?

She's busy. Could you call back later?

그녀는 통화 중인데요. 이따가 다시
전화하시겠어요?

geu-nyeo-neun tong-hwa jung-in-de-yo. i-dda-ga da-si
jeon-hwa-ha-si-ge-sseo-yo?

It's me.

바로 전데요.

ba-ro jeon-de-yo

Are you the one I spoke with a short time ago?

조금 전에 저와 통화하셨던 분인가요?

jo-geum jeo-ne jeo-wa tong-hwa-ha-syeot-ddeon
bu-nin-ga-yo?

Could you speak a little bit louder?

좀 크게 말해 줄래(요)?

jom keu-ge mal-hae jul-rae(-yo)?

Coud you lower your voice a little bit?

좀 작게 말해 줄래(요)?

jom jak-gge mal-hae jul-rae(-yo)?

Could you speak more slowly?

좀 천천히 말해 줄래(요)?

jom cheon-cheon-hi mal-hae jul-rae(-yo)?

I beg your pardon?

다시 한 번 말해 줄래(요)?

da-si han beon mal-hae jul-rae(-yo)?

I can't hear you very well.

잘 안 들려(요).

jal an deul-ryeo(-yo)

Transferring a Call

Hold on, please.

잠시 기다려 주세요.

jam-si gi-da-ryeo ju-se-yo

I'll put you through.

연결해 드리겠습니다.

yeon-gyeol-hae deu-ri-get-sseum-ni-da

The phone number you are trying to dial is busy.

연결하려는 전화번호가 통화 중이에요.

yeon-gyeol-ha-ryeo-neun jeon-hwa-beon-ho-ga tong-hwa jung-i-e-yo

Hold on and I'll get him.

기다리세요, 바꿔 드릴게요.

gi-da-ri-se-yo, ba-ggwo deu-ril-gge-yo

Hold on and I'll put you through to English speaker.

끊지 마세요, 영어 할 수 있는 분을 바꿔 드릴게요.

ggeun-chi ma-se-yo, yeong-eo hal ssu in-neun bu-neul ba-ggwo deu-ril-gge-yo

It's for you.

네 전화야.

ne jeon-hwa-ya

당신 전화예요.

dang-sin jeon-hwa-ye-yo

Ringing Back

I'll get back to you later.

다음에 전화할게(요).

da-eu-me jeon-hwa-hal-gge(-yo)

다음에 전화드릴게요.

da-eu-me jeon-hwa-deu-ril-gge-yo

Can I call you back?

제가 다시 전화드릴까요?

je-ga da-si jeon-hwa-deu-ril-gga-yo?

I'll get in touch with you soon.

제가 잠시 후에 전화드릴게요.

je-ga jam-si hu-e jeon-hwa-deu-ril-gge-yo

Please call me back in 10 minutes.

10분 후에 제가 다시 전화드리겠습니다.

sip-bbun hu-e je-ga da-si jeon-hwa-deu-ri-get-sseum-ni-da

Should I get him to call you back?

그에게 다시 전화하라고 할까(요)?

geu-e-ge da-si jeon-hwa-ha-ra-go hal-gga(-yo)?

Delaying a Call

I'm on the phone.

통화 중이에요.

tong-hwa jung-i-e-yo

He is not here now.

그는 지금 없는데(요).

geu-neun ji-geum eom-neun-de(-yo)

Sorry, he's just left.

죄송합니다만, 그는 방금 나갔습니다.

joe-song-ham-ni-da-man, geu-neun bang-geum
na-gat-sseum-ni-da

I'm a bit busy right now.

지금 좀 바빠서(요).

ji-geum jom ba-bba-seo(-yo)

It's a bit uncomfortable to talk, call you later.

지금 말하기 불편해서, 이따가 전화할게(요).

ji-geum mal-ha-gi bul-pyeon-hae-seo, i-dda-ga
jeon-hwa-hal-gge(-yo)

If anyone calls, tell them I'm not here.

전화 오면, 나 없다고 해(요).

jeon-hwa o-myeon, na eop-dda-go hae(-yo)

Messages

Can I take a message?

메시지 남기시겠어요?

me-si-ji nam-gi-si-ge-sseo-yo?

I'm sorry but he is busy.
Would you like to leave a message?

죄송합니다만, 그가 바빠서요.
메시지 남기시겠어요?

joe-song-ham-ni-da-man, geu-ga ba-bba-sseo-yo.
me-si-ji nam-gi-si-ge-sseo-yo?

Text please.

문자메시지 주세요.

mun-jja-me-si-ji ju-se-yo

Tell him to call me.

저한테 전화하라고 그에게 전해 주세요.

jeo-han-te jeon-hwa-ha-ra-go geu-e-ge jeon-hae ju-se-yo

Ask him to call me at 123-4567.

그에게 123-4567로 전화하라고 전해
주세요.

geu-e-ge il-i-sa-me sa-o-ryuk-chil-ro jeon-hwa-ha-ra-go
jeon-hae ju-se-yo

Just tell her that I called.

제가 연락했다고 그녀에게 전해 주세요.

je-ga yeol-ra-kaet-dda-go geu-nyeo-e-ge jeon-hae ju-se-yo

Wrong Numbers

You have the wrong number.

전화 잘못 거셨어요.

jeon-hwa jal-mot geo-syeo-sseo-yo

There's no one here by that name.

그런 사람 없어(요).

geu-reon sa-ram eop-sseo(-yo)

What number did you want?

어디에 전화하셨어요?

eo-di-e jeon-hwa-ha-syeo-sseo-yo?

You should double-check the number.

전화번호를 다시 확인해 보세요.

jeon-hwa-beon-ho-reul da-si hwa-gin-hae bo-se-yo

I must have the wrong number.

제가 잘못 걸었네요.

je-ga jal-mot geo-reon-ne-yo

Hanging Up

Call you soon.

곧 전화할게(요).

got jeon-hwa-hal-gge(-yo)

Thank you for calling.

전화해 주셔서 감사합니다.

jeon-hwa-hae ju-syeo-seo gam-sa-ham-ni-da

Well, I have to get off the line now.

그럼, 전화 끊어야겠어(요).

geu-reom, jeon-hwa ggeu-neo-ya-ge-sseo(-yo)

Don't forget to drop me a line.

나한테 연락하는 것 잊지 마(세요).

na-han-te yeol-ra-ka-neun geot it-jji ma(-se-yo)

Contact me anytime.

언제든지 저에게 연락하세요.

eon-je-deun-ji jeo-e-ge yeol-ra-ka-se-yo

Office Calls

Hello, Sam-dong Company, Sales Department, Jun Lee speaking.

안녕하세요, 삼동 회사 영업부, 이준입니다.

an-nyeong-ha-se-yo, sam-dong hoe-sa yeong-eop-bbu, i-jun-im-ni-da

Thank you for calling Sam-dong Company.

삼동 회사에 전화해 주셔서 감사합니다.

Sam-dong hoe-sa-e jeon-hwa-hae ju-syeo-seo
gam-sa-ham-ni-da

I'm calling about tomorrow's meeting.

내일 회의를 확인하려고 전화했습니다.

nae-il hoe-i-reul hwa-gin-ha-ryeo-go
jeon-hwa-haet-sseum-ni-da

May I speak with someone in the Personnel Department?

인사부로 돌려 주세요.

in-sa-bu-ro dol-ryeo ju-se-yo

Chapter 2

Making Conversation

Waking & Getting Up

\# You have to wake up.

일어나야 해(요).

i-reo-na-ya hae(-yo)

\# Rise and shine!

일어나, 아침이야!

i-reo-na, a-chi-mi-ya!

\# Did you get up?

일어났어(요)?

i-reo-na-sseo(-yo)?

\# I just woke up.

막 일어났어(요).

mak i-reo-na-sseo(-yo)

\# Get up now, or you'll be late.

일어나, 아니면 늦을 거야.

i-reo-na, a-ni-myeon neu-jeul ggeo-ya

It's time to get up.

일어날 시간이에요.

i-reo-nal si-ga-ni-e-yo

Why didn't you wake me up?

왜 안 깨웠어(요)?

wae an ggae-wo-sseo(-yo)?

Oh no, I overslept.

이런, 늦잠을 잤어(요).

i-reon, neut-jja-meul ja-sseo(-yo)

Please wake me up early tomorrow.

내일 아침에 일찍 깨워 줘(요).

nae-il a-chi-me il-jjik ggae-wo jwo(-yo)

I wake up early in the morning.

나는 일찍 일어나(요).

na-neun il-jjik i-reo-na(-yo)

I'm a morning person.

나는 아침형 인간이에요.

na-neun a-chim-hyeong in-ga-ni-e-yo

I usually wake up at 6 o'clock in the morning.

나는 보통 아침 6시에 일어나(요).

na-neun bo-tong a-chim yeo-seot-ssi-e i-reo-na(-yo)

Sometimes I can't wake up in the morning.

때때로 아침에 못 일어나(요).

ddae-ddae-ro a-chi-me mot i-reo-na(-yo)

I need to receive a wake-up call in the morning.

아침에 모닝콜이 필요해(요).

a-chi-me mo-ning-ko-ri pi-ryo-hae(-yo)

Washing & Brushing

Wash your hands first.

먼저 손을 씻어(요).

meon-jeo so-neul ssi-seo(-yo)

I need to wash my face to wake up.

잠을 깨려면 세수를 해야겠어(요).

ja-meul ggae-ryeo-myeon se-su-reul hae-ya-ge-sseo(-yo)

Would you bring a towel for me?

수건 좀 갖다줄래(요)?

su-geon jom gat-dda-jul-rae(-yo)?

Brush your teeth 3 times per day.

하루에 세 번 이를 닦아야 해(요).

ha-ru-e se beon i-reul da-gga-ya hae(-yo)

Don't forget to brush your teeth after eating.

식사 후에 양치하는 것 잊지 마(세요).

sik-ssa hu-e yang-chi-ha-neun geot it-jji ma(-se-yo)

Can I use this new toothbrush?

이 새 칫솔을 써도 될까(요)?

i sae chit-sso-reul sseo-do doel-gga(-yo)?

Shower & Bathing

I take a bath everyday.

나는 매일 목욕해(요).

na-neun mae-il mo-gyo-kae(-yo)

Take a bath quickly.

어서 목욕해라.

eo-seo mo-gyo-kae-ra

I need a quick shower.

서둘러 샤워해야 해(요).

seo-dul-reo sya-wo-hae-ya hae(-yo)

Taking a cold shower is good for your health.

찬물로 샤워하는 것은 건강에 좋아(요).

chan-mul-ro sya-wo-ha-neun geo-seun geon-gang-e
jo-a(-yo)

Your showers are too long.

너는 샤워를 너무 오래 해(요).

neo-neun sya-wo-reul neo-mu o-rae hae(-yo)

I take a shower every morning after jogging.

매일 아침 조깅하고 나서 샤워를 해(요).

mae-il a-chim jo-ging-ha-go na-seo sya-wo-reul hae(-yo)

Shampooing

I had no time to shampoo this morning.

아침에 머리 감을 시간이 없어(요).

a-chi-me meo-ri ga-meul si-ga-ni eop-sseo(-yo)

I make it a rule to shampoo my hair every morning.

아침에 머리 감는 습관이 있어(요).

a-chi-me meo-ri gam-neun seup-ggwa-ni i-sseo(-yo)

Last night, I was shampooing my hair when the water went off.

지난밤에, 머리를 감는데 물이 안 나왔어(요).

ji-nan-ba-me, meo-ri-reul gam-neun-de mu-ri an na-wa-sseo(-yo)

I usually shampoo in the evening because there's not enough time in the morning.

아침에 시간이 없기 때문에 보통 저녁에 머리를 감아(요).

a-chi-me si-ga-ni eop-ggi ddae-mu-ne bo-tong jeo-nyeo-ge meo-ri-reul ga-ma(-yo)

Having a Meal

Breakfast is ready!

아침 식사 준비 다 됐어(요)!

a-chim sik-ssa jun-bi da dwae-sseo(-yo)!

What should I make for breakfast?

아침 식사로 뭐 준비하지(요)?

a-chim sik-ssa-ro mwo jun-bi-ha-ji(-yo)?

I don't eat breakfast.

나는 아침 식사를 안 해(요).

na-neun a-chim sik-ssa-reul an hae(-yo)

I don't feel like having breakfast this morning.

오늘 아침은 식사할 기분이 아니에요.

o-neul a-chi-meun sik-ssa-hal gi-bu-ni a-ni-e-yo

Our meal is ready, so let's eat.

식사 준비 다 됐어, 먹자.

sik-ssa jun-bi da dwae-sseo, meok-jja

My stomach is rumbling because I didn't have breakfast yet.

아직 식사를 못 해서, 배에서 꼬르륵 소리가 나고 있어(요).

a-jik sik-ssa-reul mot hae-seo, bae-e-seo ggo-reu-reuk so-ri-ga na-go i-sseo(-yo)

Would you like to have dinner with us?

우리 같이 저녁 먹을래(요)?

u-ri ga-chi jeo-nyeok meo-geul-rae(-yo)?

What should we do for dinner?

저녁 식사로 우리 뭘 먹을까(요)?

jeo-nyeok sik-ssa-ro u-ri mwol meo-geul-gga(-yo)?

Will you come to my house for dinner?

저녁 식사하러 우리 집에 올래(요)?

jeo-nyeok sik-ssa-ha-reo u-ri ji-be ol-rae(-yo)?

Don't be picky.

편식하지 마(세요).

pyeon-si-ka-ji ma(-se-yo)

Finish up your plate.

남기지 말고 다 먹어(요).

nam-gi-ji mal-go da meo-geo(-yo)

Have you finished?

밥 다 먹었어(요)?

bap da meo-geo-sseo(-yo)?

Do you want some more rice?

밥 더 줄까(요)?

bap deo jul-gga(-yo)?

Getting Dressed

These pants are too tight.

이 바지 너무 끼어(요).

i ba-ji neo-mu ggi-eo(-yo)

I was dressed casually in jeans and T-shirt.

청바지와 티셔츠로 간편하게 입었어(요).

cheong-ba-ji-wa ti-syeo-cheu-ro gan-pyeon-ha-ge
i-beo-sseo(-yo)

Mi-hee is wearing a white blouse and a pink skirt.

미희는 하얀 블라우스에 분홍 치마를 입고 있어(요).

mi-hi-neun ha-yan beul-ra-u-seu-e bun-hong chi-ma-reul ip-ggo i-sseo(-yo)

It's cold out so put on your coat.

밖은 추우니 코트를 입어라.

ba-ggeun chu-u-ni ko-teu-reul i-beo-ra

Take off your coat and relax.

외투를 벗고 쉬어(요).

oe-tu-reul beot-ggo swi-eo(-yo)

Which tie should I wear?

어떤 넥타이를 매면 좋을까(요)?

eo-ddeon nek-ta-i-reul mae-myeon jo-eul-gga(-yo)?

That dress suits you.

그 원피스 너한테 잘 어울리는데.

geu won-pi-seu neo-han-te jal eo-ul-ri-neun-de

The blue hat doesn't really work.

파란색 모자는 정말 안 어울려(요).

pa-ran-saek mo-ja-neun jeong-mal an eo-ul-ryeo(-yo)

What should I wear today?

오늘 뭘 입으면 좋을까(요)?

o-neul mwol i-beu-myeon jo-eul-gga(-yo)?

He wears the same suit everyday.

그는 항상 같은 옷이에요.

geu-neun hang-sang ga-teun o-si-e-yo

You're dressed from head to toe.

머리부터 발끝까지 차려입었구나.

meo-ri-bu-teo bal-ggeut-gga-ji cha-ryeo-i-beot-ggu-na

Make-up

I need to put on some make-up.

화장해야 해(요).

hwa-jang-hae-ya hae(-yo)

I have no time to make-up in the morning.

아침에 화장할 시간이 없어(요).

a-chi-me hwa-jang-hal si-ga-ni eop-sseo(-yo)

You don't have to make-up.

화장 안 해도 괜찮아(요).

hwa-jang an hae-do gwaen-cha-na(-yo)

She usually spends an hour doing her face.

그녀는 보통 화장하는 데 한 시간 걸려(요).

geu-nyeo-neun bo-tong hwa-jang-ha-neun de han si-gan geol-ryeo(-yo)

You look good.

괜찮게 꾸몄는데(요).

gwaen-chan-ke ggu-myeon-neun-de(-yo)

She's up the latest fashions.

그녀는 최신 유행을 따라(요).

geu-nyeo-neun choe-sin yu-haeng-eul dda-ra(-yo)

Watching TV

What's on TV this evening?

오늘 저녁에 텔레비전에서 뭐 해(요)?

o-neul jeo-nyeo-ge tel-re-bi-jeo-ne-seo mwo hae(-yo)?

What's on the KBS?

KBS에서 뭘 방송하고 있어(요)?

ke-i-bi-e-seu-e-seo mwol bang-song-ha-go i-sseo(-yo)?

What programs do you like?

어떤 프로그램을 좋아해(요)?

eo-ddeon peu-ro-geu-rae-meul jo-a-hae(-yo)?

Let's change the channel.

채널을 바꿔라.

chae-neo-reul ba-ggwo-ra

Stop flipping channels.

채널 바꾸지 마(세요).

chae-neol ba-ggu-ji ma(-se-yo)

Hand me the remote control, please.

리모컨 좀 줘(요).

ri-mo-keon jom jwo(-yo)

Going to Bed

It's time to go to bed.

잘 시간이야.

jal si-ga-ni-ya

I have to go to bed.

자러 가야겠어(요).

ja-reo ga-ya-ge-sseo(-yo)

Are you still up?

아직 안 자(요)?

a-jik an ja(-yo)?

It's almost midnight.

벌써 한밤중이야.

beol-sseo han-bam-jung-i-ya

Will you turn off the light?

불 좀 꺼 줄래(요)?

bul jom ggeo jul-rae(-yo)?

Do you need another blanket?

담요를 더 드릴까요?

dam-nyo-reul deo deu-ril-gga-yo?

Don't use your cell phone in bed.

잠자리에서 휴대폰 하지 마(세요).

jam-jja-ri-e-seo hyu-dae-pon ha-ji ma(-se-yo)

Sleeping Habits

My husband has a bad sleeping habit.

남편의 잠버릇은 좋지 않아(요).

nam-pyeo-ne jam-bbeo-reu-seun jo-chi a-na(-yo)

My wife tosses and turns a lot in her sleep.

아내는 자면서 자꾸 뒤척여(요).

a-nae-neun ja-myeon-seo ja-ggu dwi-cheo-gyeo(-yo)

You snored like a bulldog last night.

넌 간밤에 코를 엄청 골았어(요).

neon gan-ba-me ko-reul eom-cheong go-ra-sseo(-yo)

He started snoring as soon as he fell asleep.

그는 잠들자마자 코를 골기 시작했어(요).

geu-neun jam-deul-ja-ma-ja ko-reul gol-gi si-ja-kae-sseo(-yo)

Jeong-won talks in her sleep.

정원이는 잘 때 잠꼬대를 해(요).

jeong-wo-ni-neun jal ddae jam-ggo-dae-reul hae(-yo)

He grinds his teeth in bed.

그는 잘 때 이를 갈아(요).

geu-neun jal ddae i-reul ga-ra(-yo)

Deep Sleep

I slept well last night.

어젯밤에 푹 잤어(요).

eo-jet-bba-me puk ja-sseo(-yo)

We all fell asleep so fast.

우리 모두 금방 곯아떨어졌어(요).

u-ri mo-du geum-bang go-ra-ddeo-reo-jeo-sseo(-yo)

I didn't sleep well.

그다지 잘 자지 못했어(요).

geu-da-ji jal ja-ji mo-tae-sseo(-yo)

Did you have a bad sleep?

잘 못 잤어(요)?

jal mot ja-sseo(-yo)?

I haven't been getting much sleep lately.

요즘 잠을 잘 못 자(요).

yo-jeum ja-meul jal mot ja(-yo)

You'll feel better after a good sleep.

잘 자고 나면 훨씬 좋아질 거예요.

jal ja-go na-myeon hwol-ssin jo-a-jil ggeo-ye-yo

Dreaming

Sweet dreams!

좋은 꿈 꿔(요)!

jo-eun ggum ggwo(-yo)!

I dream of him from time to time.

가끔 그의 꿈을 꿔(요).

ga-ggeum geu-e ggu-meul ggwo(-yo)

If you dream of pigs, you should buy a lottery ticket!

돼지꿈을 꾸면, 복권을 사(세요)!

dwae-ji-ggu-meul ggu-myeon, bok-ggwo-neul sa(-se-yo)!

I had a strange dream last night.

어제 이상한 꿈을 꿨어(요).

eo-je i-sang-han ggu-meul ggwo-sseo(-yo)

I had a nightmare.

악몽을 꿨어(요).

ang-mong-eul ggwo-sseo(-yo)

I had a nightmare, so I couldn't get back to sleep.

악몽을 꿔서, 다시 잠들 수 없었어(요).

ang-mong-eul ggwo-seo, da-si jam-deul ssu
eop-sseo-sseo(-yo)

The Restroom

Where is the restroom?

화장실이 어디 있어(요)?

hwa-jang-si-ri eo-di i-sseo(-yo)?

Nature is calling.

화장실에 다녀올게(요).

hwa-jang-si-re da-nyeo-ol-gge(-yo)

Someone is in the restroom.

화장실에 누가 있어(요).

hwa-jang-si-re nu-ga i-sseo(-yo)

Can I use the toilet?

화장실 좀 써도 돼(요)?

hwa-jang-sil jom sseo-do dwae(-yo)?

I have to go to the bathroom first.

화장실 좀 먼저 가야겠어(요).

hwa-jang-sil jom meon-jeo ga-ya-ge-sseo(-yo)

123

The bathroom is right next to my room.

화장실은 내 방 바로 옆에 있어(요).

hwa-jang-si-reun nae bang ba-ro yeo-pe i-sseo(-yo)

Toilet Manners

You should flush the toilet.

변기 물을 꼭 내리세요.

byeon-gi mu-reul ggok nae-ri-se-yo

Please put your toilet paper in the toilet.

화장실 휴지는 변기에 버리세요.

hwa-jang-sil hyu-ji-neun byeon-gi-e beo-ri-se-yo

Put the sanatary napkin in the trash can.

생리대는 휴지통에 버리세요.

saeng-ri-dae-neun hyu-ji-tong-e beo-ri-se-yo

Don't make a mess.

어지르지 마(세요).

eo-ji-reu-ji ma(-se-yo)

Don't spit on the floor.

바닥에 침을 뱉지 마(세요).

ba-da-ge chi-meul baet-jji ma(-se-yo)

Don't talk on the big white phone.

변기에 토하지 마(세요).

byeon-gi-e to-ha-ji ma(-se-yo)

The Call of Nature

I have to go and pee.

소변 보러 가야겠어(요).

so-byeon bo-reo ga-ya-ge-sseo(-yo)

오줌 누러 가야겠어(요).

o-jum nu-reo ga-ya-ge-sseo(-yo)

쉬하러 가야겠어.

swi-ha-reo ga-ya-ge-sseo

I have a bowel movement.

대변을 보고 싶어(요).

dae-byeo-neul bo-go si-peo(-yo)

대변이 마려워(요).

dae-byeo-ni ma-ryeo-wo(-yo)

똥 마려워.

ddong ma-ryeo-wo

I can't hold it any longer!

더 이상 참을 수 없어(요)!

deo i-sang cha-meul ssu eop-sseo(-yo)!

I just pinched a loaf.

화장실에서 대변을 봤어(요).

hwa-jang-si-re-seo dae-byeo-neul bwa-sseo(-yo)

I haven't had a bowel movement.

대변을 보지 못했어(요).

dae-byeo-neul bo-ji mo-tae-sseo(-yo)

Toilet Issues

The toilet doesn't flush properly.

변기가 제대로 안 내려가(요).

byeon-gi-ga je-dae-ro an nae-ryeo-ga(-yo)

The toilet bowl is clogged.

변기가 막혔어(요).

byeon-gi-ga ma-kyeo-sseo(-yo)

The bathroom light doesn't work.

욕실 전등이 고장 났어(요).

yok-ssil jeon-deung-i go-jang na-sseo(-yo)

The bathroom's light doesn't turn on.

욕실의 전등이 안 켜져(요).

yok-ssi-re jeon-deung-i an kyeo-jeo(-yo)

The tap is leaking.

수도꼭지가 새(요).

su-do-ggok-jji-ga sae(-yo)

There is no toilet paper in the bathroom.

화장실에 휴지가 없어(요).

hwa-jang-si-re hyu-ji-ga eop-sseo(-yo)

The Living Room

After dinner, we all have tea in the living room.

저녁 식사 후, 우리 모두 거실에서 차를 마셔(요).

jeo-nyeok sik-ssa hu, u-ri mo-du geo-si-re-seo cha-reul ma-syeo(-yo)

I need a more spacious living room.

거실이 좀 더 넓으면 좋겠어(요).

geo-si-ri jom deo neol-beu-myeon jo-ke-sseo(-yo)

There is no TV in the living room.

거실에 TV가 없어(요).

geo-si-re ti-bi-ga eop-sseo(-yo)

The living room is a mess.

거실이 엉망이에요.

geo-si-ri eong-mang-i-e-yo

We need to redo the entire living room.

거실 전체를 다시 꾸며야겠어(요).

geo-sil jeon-che-reul da-si ggu-myeo-ya-ge-sseo(-yo)

The Refrigerator

I'll put the leftovers in the fridge.

남은 음식은 냉장고에 있어(요).

na-meun eum-si-geun naeng-jang-go-e i-sseo(-yo)

The refrigerator is open. Close the door, please.

냉장고 문이 열려 있네(요). 문 좀 닫아 줘(요).

naeng-jang-go mu-ni yeol-ryeo in-ne(-yo). mun jom da-da jwo(-yo)

My refrigerator is full of junk food.

우리 집 냉장고는 가공식품으로 가득해(요).

u-ri jip naeng-jang-go-neun ga-gong-sik-pu-meu-ro ga deu-kae(-yo)

What's the volume of this refrigerator?

이 냉장고의 용량은 얼마예요?

i naeng-jang-go-e yong-nyang-eun eol-ma-ye-yo?

The fridge was unplugged so the ice melted.

냉장고 코드가 빠져 있어서 얼음이 녹았어(요).

naeng-jang-go ko-deu-ga bba-jeo i-sseo-seo eo-reu-mi no-ga-sseo(-yo)

Preparing Meals

I'm in the middle of making dinner.

저녁 식사를 준비하고 있어(요).

jeo-nyeok sik-ssa-reul jun-bi-ha-go i-sseo(-yo)

What shall we have for dinner?

오늘 저녁에 뭐 먹을까(요)?

o-neul jeo-nyeo-ge mwo meo-geul-gga(-yo)?

It's almost ready. Just a minute.

거의 다 됐어요. 잠시 기다려 주세요.

geo-i da dwae-sseo-yo. jam-si gi-da-ryeo ju-se-yo

Dinner will be ready in about 10 minutes.

10분쯤이면 저녁이 다 준비돼(요).

sip-bbun-jjeu-mi-myeon jeo-nyeo-gi da jun-bi-dwae(-yo)

Will you help me set the table?

식탁 차리는 것을 좀 도와줄래(요)?

sik-tak cha-ri-neun geo-seul jom do-wa-jul-rae(-yo)?

Cooking

She cooked it until the water boiled away.

그녀는 물이 졸아들 때까지 조리했어(요).

geu-nyeo-neun mu-ri jo-ra-deul ddae-gga-ji
jo-ri-hae-sseo(-yo)

I made your favorite.

네가 좋아하는 걸 만들었어(요).

ne-ga jo-a-ha-neun geol man-deu-reo-sseo(-yo)

I've prepared bulgogi for dinner.

저녁 식사로 불고기를 준비했어(요).

jeo-nyeok sik-ssa-ro bul-go-gi-reul jun-bi-hae-sseo(-yo)

The delicous cooking smell make my mouth water.

음식 냄새 때문에 군침이 돌아(요).

eum-sik naem-sae ddae-mu-ne gun-chi-mi do-ra(-yo)

How does it taste?

맛 어때(요)?

mat eo-ddae(-yo)?

Help yourself.

맛있게 드세요.

ma-dit-gge deu-se-yo

Recipes

\# Would you mind sharing the recipe?

이 요리 어떻게 만들었는지 알려 줄 수 있어(요)?

i yo-ri eo-ddeo-ke man-deu-reon-neun-ji al-ryeo jul ssu i-sseo(-yo)?

\# I just use my mom's old recipe.

엄마가 쓰던 요리법대로 했을 뿐이에요.

eom-ma-ga sseu-deon yo-ri-bbeop-ddae-ro hae-sseul bbu-ni-e-yo

\# Just follow the steps in this recipe.

이 요리법대로 따라 하세요.

i yo-ri-bboep-ddae-ro dda-ra ha-se-yo

\# Can I borrow that japchae recipe?

잡채 레시피 좀 알려 줄래(요)?

jap-chae re-si-pi jom al-ryeo jul-rae(-yo)?

What do you think about my new recipe?

내 새로운 레시피 어때(요)?

nae sae-ro-un re-si-pi eo-ddae(-yo)?

Doing the Dishes

Put your dishes in the sink.

그릇을 개수대에 넣어 주세요.

geu-reu-seul gae-su-dae-e neo-eo ju-se-yo

Could you clear the table and load the dishwasher?

식탁을 다 치우고 그릇을 식기세척기에 넣어 줄래(요)?

sik-ta-geul da chi-u-go geu-reu-seul sik-ggi-se-cheok-ggi-e
neo-eo jul-rae(-yo)?

I'll do the dishes.

내가 설거지 할게(요).

nae-ga seol-geo-ji hal-gge(-yo)

He said that he'd help me do the dishes.

그는 설거지를 도와준다고 (말)했어(요).

geu-neun seol-geo-ji-reul do-wa-jun-da-go
(mal-)hae-sseo(-yo)

I'll do the dishes since you cooked dinner.

당신이 저녁을 했으니, 설거지는 제가
할게요.

dang-si-ni jeo-nyeo-geul hae-sseu-ni, seol-geo-ji-neun je-ga
hal-gge-yo

Kitchenware

The kitchen in this apartment is fully
equipped.

이 아파트의 부엌은 모든 설비가 잘 갖춰져
있어(요).

i a-pa-teu-e bu-eo-keun mo-deun seol-bi-ga jal ga-chwo-jeo
i-sseo(-yo)

The pans are arranged neatly in the cupboard.

그 냄비들은 찬장에 가지런히 있어(요).

geu naem-bi-deu-reun chan-jjang-e ga-ji-reon-hi i-sseo(-yo)

Your kitchen is so organizied!

부엌이 잘 정리되어 있군(요)!

bu-eo-ki jal jeong-ri-doe-eo it-ggun(-yo)!

You should handle those bowls with care.

이 식기들을 주의해 주세요.

i sik-ggi-deu-reul ju-i-hae ju-se-yo

The longer you use a frying pan, the better it becomes for cooking.

프라이팬은 오래 쓸수록 길들여져서 쓰기 좋아(요).

peu-ra-i-pae-neun o-rae sseul-ssu-rok gil-deu-ryeo-jeo-seo sseu-gi jo-a(-yo)

Ranges

A microwave is a necessity in modern life.

전자레인지는 현대 생활의 필수품이죠.

jeon-ja-re-in-ji-neun hyeon-dae saeng-hwa-re
pil-ssu-pu-mi-jyo

A microwave can reduce the time to cook.

전자레인지는 조리 시간을 줄여 줘(요).

jeon-ja-re-in-ji-neun jo-ri si-ga-neul ju-ryeo jwo(-yo)

You shouldn't put metal in the microwave.

전자레인지는 금속을 넣으면 안 돼요.

jeon-ja-re-in-ji-neun geum-so-geul neo-eu-myeon an
dwae-yo

One of those burners doesn't work.

가스레인지 중 하나가 작동을 안 해(요).

ga-seu-re-in-ji jung ha-na-ga jak-ddong-eul an hae(-yo)

That stove has a gas leak.

가스레인지에서 가스가 새(요).

ga-seu-re-in-ji-e-seo ga-seu-ga sae(-yo)

Table Manners

I enjoyed the meal.

잘 먹었어(요).

jal meo-geo-sseo(-yo)

잘 먹었습니다.

jal meo-geot-sseum-ni-da

Wash your hands before the meal.

밥 먹기 전에 손을 씻어라.

bap meok-ggi jeo-ne so-neul ssi-seo-ra

Don't talk with your mouth full.

입에 밥이 있을 때 말하지 마(세요).

i-be ba-bi i-sseul ddae mal-ha-ji ma(-se-yo)

You should clean your plate.

밥을 남기지 마(세요).

ba-beul nam-gi-ji ma(-se-yo)

Don't put your elbows on the table.

팔꿈치를 식탁 위에 올려놓지 마(세요).

pal-ggum-chi-reul sik-tak wi-e ol-ryeo-no-chi ma(-se-yo)

138

Put the cell phone away at the table.

식탁에서 휴대폰을 치워라.

sik-ta-ge-seo hyu-dae-po-neul chi-wo-ra

Personal Hygiene

Be extra careful about personal hygiene.

특히 개인 위생에 신경 쓰세요.

teu-ki gae-in wi-saeng-e sin-gyeong sseu-se-yo

She always washes her hands when she gets home.

그녀는 집에 돌아오면 항상 손을 먼저 씻어(요).

geu-nyeo-neun ji-be do-ra-o-myeon hang-sang so-neul meon-jeo ssi-seo(-yo)

Wash your hands to prevent the spread of germs.

세균이 퍼지지 않도록 손을 씻어라.

se-gyu-ni peo-ji-ji an-to-rok so-neul ssi-seo-ra

They have no sense of hygiene.

그들은 위생 관념이 없어(요).

geu-deu-reun wi-saeng gwan-nyeo-mi eop-sseo(-yo)

She's obsessed with neatness.

그녀는 결벽증이 있어(요).

geu-nyeo-neun gyeol-byeok-jjeung-i i-sseo(-yo)

Cleaning

I have to vacuum.

(진공)청소기로 청소해야 해(요).

(jin-gong-)cheong-so-gi-ro cheong-so-hae-ya hae(-yo)

Can you dust the shelves?

선반의 먼지 좀 털어 줄래(요)?

seon-ba-ne meon-ji jom teo-reo jul-rae(-yo)?

I clean my room everyday.

매일 방 청소를 해(요).

mae-il bang cheong-so-reul hae(-yo)

You are responsible for sweeping.

청소는 원래 네 일이잖아(요).

cheong-so-neun won-rae ne i-ri-ja-na(-yo)

Your room is so messy. Tidy it up!

방이 어질러졌구나. 정리 좀 하자!

bang-i eo-jil-reo-jeot-ggu-na. jeong-ri jom ha-ja!

Clean every nook and corner.

구석구석 깨끗이 청소해라.

gu-seok-ggu-seok ggae-ggeu-si cheong-so-hae-ra

Start cleaning here.

여기부터 청소합시다.

yeo-gi-bu-teo cheong-so-hap-ssi-da

We all cleaned the house together.

우리는 함께 대청소를 했어(요).

u-ri-neun ham-gge dae-cheong-so-reul hae-sseo(-yo)

I clean the house from cellar to rafters once a month.

매달 한 번 대청소를 해(요).

mae-dal han beon dae-cheong-so-reul hae(-yo)

Please help me clean.

청소하는 걸 도와주세요.

cheong-so-ha-neun geol do-wa-ju-se-yo

Since I swept the floor, would you mop it?

내가 바닥을 청소했으니, 네가 걸레질 할래(요)?

nae-ga ba-da-geul cheong-so-hae-sseu-ni, ne-ga geol-re-jil hal-rae(-yo)?

I want my house clean without cleaning it.

청소하지 않아도 집이 깨끗하면 좋겠어(요).

cheong-so-ha-ji a-na-do ji-bi ggae-ggeu-ta-myeon jo-ke-sseo(-yo)

Trash & Recycling

Why didn't you put out the trash?

왜 쓰레기를 안 버렸어(요)?

wae sseu-re-gi-reul an beo-ryeo-sseo(-yo)?

Would you take out the garbage?

쓰레기 좀 버려 줄래(요)?

sseu-re-gi jom beo-ryeo jul-rae(-yo)?

Did you put out the garbage last night?

어젯밤에 쓰레기 내다 놨어(요)?

eo-jet-bba-me sseu-re-gi nae-da nwa-sseo(-yo)?

You should separate the garbage before disposing of it.

쓰레기는 분류해서 버려야 해(요).

sseu-re-gi-neun bul-ryu-hae-seo beo-ryeo-ya hae(-yo)

When is garbage day?

쓰레기 수거일은 언제예요?

sseu-re-gi su-geo-i-reun eon-je-ye-yo?

Where should I put the recyclables?

재활용 쓰레기는 어디에 버려야 해(요)?

jae-hwa-ryong sseu-re-gi-neun eo-di-e beo-ryeo-ya hae(-yo)?

Doing the Wash

\# I need to do my laundry today.

오늘 빨래해야 해(요).

o-neul bbal-rae-hae-ya hae(-yo)

\# I'll run the washing machine.

세탁기를 돌려야겠어(요).

se-tak-ggi-reul dol-ryeo-ya-ge-sseo(-yo)

\# Put the laundry into the washing machine.

빨래를 세탁기에 넣어라.

bbal-rae-reul se-tak-ggi-e neo-eo-ra

\# How much detergent do I need?

세제를 얼마나 넣어(요)?

se-je-reul eol-ma-na neo-eo(-yo)?

Don't mix whites and colors.

하얀 옷하고 색깔 옷을 섞지 마(세요).

ha-yan o-ta-go saek-ggal o-seul seok-jji ma(-se-yo)

This sweater can't be washed in hot water.

이 스웨터는 뜨거운 물에 빨 수 없어(요).

i seu-we-teo-neun ddeu-geo-un mu-re bbal ssu
eop-sseo(-yo)

When it is sunny, the laundry dries in no
time.

날씨가 좋으면, 빨래가 빨리 말라(요).

nal-ssi-ga jo-eu-myeon, bbal-rae-ga bbal-ri mal-ra(-yo)

Did you hang the laundry up to dry?

옷을 잘 널었어(요)?

o-seul jal neo-reo-sseo(-yo)?

I forgot to put up the clothes up to dry.

옷 너는 걸 잊어버렸어(요).

ot neo-neun geol i-jeo-beo-ryeo-sseo(-yo)

Please help me fold up the clothes.

옷 개는 거 좀 도와줄래(요)?

ot gae-neun geo jom do-wa-jul-rae(-yo)?

Will you iron the shirts?

셔츠 다려 줄래(요)?

syeo-cheu da-ryeo jul-rae(-yo)?

Interior Design

I like furnishing houses.

집 꾸미는 걸 좋아해(요).

jip ggu-mi-neun geol jo-a-hae(-yo)

I'm interested in architecture and furniture design.

인테리어와 가구 디자인에 관심이 많아(요).

in-te-ri-eo-wa ga-gu-di-ja-i-ne gwan-si-mi ma-na(-yo)

I don't like the interior design of my new house.

새 집 인테리어가 마음에 안 들어(요).

sae jip in-te-ri-eo-ga ma-eu-me an deu-reo(-yo)

The new curtains don't match the color of the walls.

새 커튼은 벽 색깔과 어울리지 않아(요).

sae keo-teu-neun byeok saek-ggal-gwa eo-ul-ri-ji a-na(-yo)

The interior's a bit old-fashioned.

거실의 인테리어가 좀 구식이에요.

geo-si-re in-te-ri-eo-ga jom gu-si-gi-e-yo

Driving

I got my driver's license last week.

지난주에 운전면허를 땄어(요).

ji-nan-ju-e un-jeon-myeon-heo-reul dda-sseo(-yo)

I can't drive very well.

운전을 잘 못해(요).

un-jeo-neul jal mo-tae(-yo)

My driver's license expires next month.

내 운전면허증은 다음 달이 만기예요.

nae un-jeon-myeon-heo-jjeung-eun da-eum da-ri
man-gi-ye-yo

I recently renewed my driver's license.

최근에 운전면허증을 갱신했어(요).

choe-geu-ne un-jeon-myeon-heo-jjeung-eul
gaeng-sin-hae-sseo(-yo)

He had his license revoked for drunk driving.

그는 음주운전 사고로 운전면허가
취소됐어(요).

geu-neun eum-ju-un-jeon sa-go-ro un-jeon-myeon-heo-ga
chwi-so-dwae-sseo(-yo)

You're driving too fast. Slow down!

너무 빨라(요). 속도를 줄여(요)!

neo-mu bbal-ra(-yo). sok-ddo-reul ju-ryeo(-yo)!

Watch out! That's a red light!

조심해요! 빨간 불이에요!

jo-sim-hae-yo! bbal-gan bu-ri-e-yo!

Fasten your seat belt.

안전벨트를 매(세요).

an-jeon-bel-teu-reul mae(-se-yo)

Go straight and turn right at the lights.

직진한 다음 신호등에서 우회전해(요).

jik-jjin-han da-eum sin-ho-deung-e-seo u-hoe-jeon-hae(-yo)

Do you mind if I drive?

내가 교대로 운전해 줄까(요)?

nae-ga gyo-dae-ro un-jeon-hae jul-gga(-yo)?

Are you sure this is the right road?

이 길로 가는 게 맞아(요)?

i gil-ro ga-neun ge ma-ja(-yo)?

He knows a lot about cars.

그는 차에 대해 많이 알아(요).

geu-neun cha-e dae-hae ma-ni a-ra(-yo)

Parking

Where is the parking lot?

주차장이 어디예요?

ju-cha-jang-i eo-di-ye-yo?

Can I park here?

여기에 주차해도 돼요?

yeo-gi-e ju-cha-hae-do dwae-yo?

There is a parking lot behind the building.

이 건물 뒤에 주차장이 있어(요).

i geon-mul dwi-e ju-cha-jang-i i-sseo(-yo)

There is no space to park here.

여기에 자리가 없어(요).

yeo-gi-e ja-ri-ga eop-sseo(-yo)

How much is it per hour for parking?

시간당 주차비가 얼마예요?

si-gan-dang ju-cha-bi-ga eol-ma-ye-yo?

Is parking free?

무료 주차예요?

mu-ryo ju-cha-ye-yo?

No parking.

주차 금지.

ju-cha geum-ji

Traffic

I got caught in traffic.

길이 심하게 막혀(요).

gi-ri sim-ha-ge ma-kyeo(-yo)

The traffic is really bad today.

오늘 교통은 심하게 막혀(요).

o-neul gyo-tong-eun sim-ha-ge ma-kyeo(-yo)

What's the hold up ahaed?

앞에 차가 왜 막히지(요)?

a-pe cha-ga wae ma-ki-ji(-yo)?

There must be an accident up ahead.

앞에서 교통사고가 난 것 같은데(요).

a-pe-seo gyo-tong-sa-go-ga nan geot ga-teun-de(-yo)

The traffic on this street is always heavy.

이 길은 항상 막혀(요).

i gi-reun hang-sang ma-kyeo(-yo)

I hate rush hour.

러시아워는 너무 싫어(요).

reo-si-a-wo-neun neo-mu si-reo(-yo)

Traffic Offenses

Pull over to the right.

오른쪽으로 차를 세워 주세요.

o-reun-jjo-geu-ro cha-reul se-wo ju-se-yo

May I see your driver's license?

운전면허증을 좀 보여 주세요.

un-jeon-myeon-heo-jjeung-eul jom bo-yeo ju-se-yo

Step out of the car, please.

차에서 내리세요.

cha-e-seo nae-ri-se-yo

Please blow into this breathalyzer.

음주측정기를 불어 주세요.

eum-ju-cheuk-jjeong-gi-reul bu-reo ju-se-yo

You were driving over the speed limit.
제한 속도를 위반하셨어요.

je-han sok-ddo-reul wi-ban-ha-syeo-sseo-yo

You didn't stop for the red light.
정지 신호에서 멈추지 않았어(요).

jeong-ji sin-ho-e-seo meom-chu-ji a-na-sseo(-yo)

Have you ever been stopped for speeding?
속도위반으로 걸린 적 있어(요)?

sok-ddo-wi-ba-neu-ro geol-rin jeok i-sseo(-yo)?

How much is the fine?
벌금은 얼마예요?

beol-geu-meun eol-ma-ye-yo?

I got a parking ticket.
주차위반 딱지를 받았어(요).

ju-cha-wi-ban ddak-jji-reul ba-da-sseo(-yo)

You shouldn't jaywalk.
무단횡단을 하면 안 됩니다.

mu-dan-hoeng-da-neul ha-myeon an doem-ni-da

This lane is left-turns only.

이 차선은 좌회전 전용입니다.

i cha-seo-neun jwa-hoe-jeon jeo-nyong-im-ni-da

This is a one-way street.

여기는 일방통행입니다.

yeo-gi-neun il-bang-tong-haeng-im-ni-da

House Hunting

I'm looking for a new house.

새 집을 찾고 있어(요).

sae ji-beul chat-ggo i-sseo(-yo)

Could you recommend some places?

추천해 줄 곳이 있어(요)?

chu-cheon-hae jul go-si i-sseo(-yo)?

How big a place are you looking for?

얼마나 큰 집을 찾으세요?

eol-ma-na keun ji-beul cha-jeu-se-yo?

Do you have something close to a subway station?

지하철역에서 좀 가까운 집이 있어(요)?

ji-ha-cheol-ryeo-ge-seo jom ga-gga-un ji-bi i-sseo(-yo)?

How many rooms does this apartment have?

이 아파트는 방이 몇 개예요?

i a-pa-teu-neun bang-i myeot gae-ye-yo?

I'd like a two-bedroom apartment.

방 두 개짜리 아파트를 원해(요).

bang du gae-jja-ri a-pa-teu-reul won-hae(-yo)

What's the public transportation like?

대중교통은 어때(요)?

dae-jung-gyo-tong-eun eo-ddae(-yo)?

It's just 10 minutes' walk from the subway.

지하철역까지 걸어서 10분밖에 안 걸려(요).

ji-ha-cheol-ryeok-gga-ji geo-reo-seo sip-bbun-ba-gge an geol-ryeo(-yo)

What floor is it on?

집이 몇 층이에요?

ji-bi myeot cheung-i-e-yo?

How much is the rent?

방세가 얼마예요?

bang-sse-ga eol-ma-ye-yo?

The rental fee is sky-high in my area.

우리 동네는 집세가 아주 비싸(요).

u-ri dong-ne-neun jip-sse-ga a-ju bi-ssa(-yo)

How long is the lease?

임대 기간은 언제까지예요?

im-dae gi-ga-neun eon-je-gga-ji-ye-yo?

Housing Contracts

I want to sign the lease.

계약하겠어요.

gye-ya-ka-ge-sseo-yo

When does the landlord come?

집주인이 언제 오세요?

jip-jju-i-ni eon-je o-se-yo?

Your rent is due on the 1st of each month.

월세는 매월 1일에 냅니다.

wol-sse-neun mae-wol i-ri-re naem-ni-da

It's 500,000 won a month. Utilities are included.

임대료는 한 달에 50만 원입니다.
공과금 포함입니다.

im-dae-ryo-neun han da-re o-sim-man wo-nim-ni-da.
gong-gwa-geum po-ha-mim-ni-da

You'll have to pay 6 months' rent in advance.

6개월치 집세를 선불로 내야 합니다.

yuk-ggae-wol-chi jip-sse-reul seon-bul-ro nae-ya ham-ni-da

When can I move in?

제가 언제 입주할 수 있어요?

je-ga eon-je ip-jju-hal ssu i-sseo-yo?

Packing

Are you all packed?

이삿짐을 다 정리했어(요)?

i-sat-jji-meul da jeong-ri-hae-sseo(-yo)?

I have to pack everything before moving.

이사 전에 짐을 다 싸야 해(요).

i-sa jeo-ne ji-meul da ssa-ya hae(-yo)

We usually rent a moving van.

우리는 보통 이삿짐차를 빌려(요).

u-ri-neun bo-tong i-sat-jjim-cha-reul bil-ryeo(-yo)

If you need any help moving, let me know.

이사할 때 도움이 필요하면, 언제든지 말해(요).

i-sa-hal ddae do-u-mi pi-ryo-ha-myeon, eon-je-deun-ji mal-hae(-yo)

We often move by the packing transportation.

보통 포장이사로 이사해(요).

bo-tong po-jang-i-sa-ro i-sa-hae(-yo)

Do you know any reliable moving companies?

믿을 만한 이삿짐센터 알고 있어(요)?

mi-deul man-han i-sat-jjim-sen-teo al-go i-sseo(-yo)?

Moving

\# I'm worried about the expense of moving.

이사 비용이 골치 아파(요).

i-sa bi-yong-i gol-chi a-pa(-yo)

\# I will sell some of my belongings before I move out.

이사 가기 전에 물건들을 팔아야겠어(요).

i-sa ga-gi jeo-ne mul-geon-deu-reul pa-ra-ya-ge-sseo(-yo)

\# I hear you're moving soon.

곧 이사 간다면서(요).

got i-sa gan-da-myeon-seo(-yo)

\# My family is planning to move houses in a month.

우리 가족은 한 달 후 이사할 계획이에요.

u-ri ga-jo-geun han dal hu i-sa-hal gye-hoe-gi-e-yo

My studio is too small. I'm moving to a two-bedroom apartment.

내 원룸은 너무 작아요. 방 두 개짜리 아파트로 이사할 기에요.

nae won-ru-meun neo-mu ja-ga-yo. bang du gae-jja-ri a-pa-teu-ro i-sa-hal ggeo-ye-yo

Can you give me a hand to put my things in order?

짐 정리하는 것을 도와줄 수 있어(요)?

jim jeong-ri-ha-neun geo-seul do-wa-jul ssu i-sseo(-yo)?

When will they turn on the gas?

언제 가스가 되나요?

eon-je ga-seu-ga doe-na-yo?

Are pets allowed?

반려동물 키울 수 있나요?

bal-ryeo-dong-mul ki-ul ssu in-na-yo?

Is Wi-Fi included?

와이파이가 포함되어 있나요?

wa-i-pa-i-ga po-ham-doe-eo in-na-yo?

Can you tell me where the nearest supermarket?

집에서 가장 가까운 슈퍼마켓은 어디예요?

ji-be-seo ga-jang ga-gga-un syu-peo-ma-ke-seun
eo-di-ye-yo?

Is this a safe neigborhood?

여기는 안전한 동네인가요?

yeo-gi-neun an-jeon-han dong-ne-in-ga-yo?

House Warming

Let me invite you to my new home this weekend.

이번 주말에 우리 새 집에 초대할게(요).

i-beon ju-ma-re u-ri sae ji-be cho-dae-hal-gge(-yo)

When is the house-warming party?

언제 집들이 해(요)?

eon-je jip-ddeu-ri hae(-yo)?

What should I bring to a house-warming party?

집들이에 뭘 가져가야 하지(요)?

jip-ddeu-ri-e mwol ga-jeo-ga-ya ha-ji(-yo)?

They will have a house-warming party tomorrow.

내일 그들은 집들이를 해(요).

nae-il geu-deu-reun jip-ddeu-ri-reul hae(-yo)

I was invited to their house-warming party.

그의 집들이 초대를 받았어(요).

geu-e jip-ddeu-ri cho-dae-reul ba-da-sseo(-yo)

Chapter 3

Out & About

Recommending Restaurants

I'd like to have a light meal.

간단하게 먹고 싶은데(요).

gan-dan-ha-ge meok-ggo si-peun-de(-yo)

Is there a good restaurant around here?

이 근처에 맛있는 음식점 있어(요)?

i geun-cheo-e ma-din-neun eum-sik-jjeom i-sseo(-yo)?

Would you recommend a nice restaurant?

괜찮은 음식점을 추천해 주세요.

gwaen-cha-neun eum-sik-jjeo-meul chu-cheon-hae ju-se-yo

Is there a restaurant open at this time?

이 시간에 문을 연 음식점이 있어(요)?

i si-ga-ne mu-neul yeon eum-sik-jjeo-mi i-sseo(-yo)?

Where is the main area for restaurants?

음식점이 많은 곳이 어디예요?

eum-sik-jjeo-mi ma-neun go-si eo-di-ye-yo?

Reservations

\# Shall I book a table at the restaurant?

음식점을 예약할까(요)?

eum-sik-jjeo-meul ye-ya-kal-gga(-yo)?

\# I'll make a reservation.

예약할게(요).

ye-ya-kal-gge(-yo)

\# Do we need a reservation?

예약해야 해(요)?

ye-ya-kae-ya hae(-yo)?

\# I'd like a table for three at 7 o'clock.

7시에 3인석 예약하려고(요).

il-gop-ssi-e sa-min-seok ye-ya-ka-ryeo-go(-yo)

\# I want to change my reservation.

예약을 바꿔 주세요.

ye-ya-geul ba-ggwo ju-se-yo

Cancel my reservation, please.

예약을 취소해 주세요.

ye-yak-geul chwi-so-hae ju-se-yo

Getting a Table

How large is your party?

몇 분이세요?

meot bu-ni-se-yo?

We have a party of 5.

다섯 명입니다.

da-seot myeong-im-ni-da

Those tables are reserved.

그 테이블들은 예약석입니다.

geu te-i-beul-deu-reun ye-yak-sseo-gim-ni-da

I'm afaraid no tables are available now.

죄송하지만, 지금은 자리가 없습니다.

joe-song-ha-ji-man, ji-geu-meun ja-ri-ga eop-sseum-ni-da

About how long will we have to wait?

얼마나 기다려야 해(요)?

eol-ma-na gi-da-ryeo-ya hae(-yo)?

There's a 20-minute wait.

20분 정도 기다리셔야 합니다.

i-sip-bbun jeong-do gi-da-ri-syeo-ya ham-ni-da

The Menu

Can I see the menu, please?

메뉴 좀 볼 수 있어요?

me-nyu jom bol ssu i-sseo(-yo)?

What would you recommend?

추천 메뉴가 뭐예요?

chu-cheon me-nyu-ga mwo-ye-yo?

We need a little more time to look at the menu.

메뉴를 좀 더 보고 싶은데요.

me-nyu-reul jom deo bo-go si-peun-de(-yo)

Could you take our orders a little later?

이따가 주문할게요.

i-dda-ga ju-mun-hal-gge-yo

What's the specialty of the house?

여기 특선 요리는 뭔가요?

yeo-gi teuk-sseon yo-ri-neun mwon-ga-yo?

We specialize in beoseot-jeongol.

버섯전골은 우리 가게의 간판 메뉴입니다.

beo-seot-jjeon-go-reun u-ri ga-ge-e gan-pan
me-nyu-im-ni-da

Ordering

Have you been served?

주문하시겠어요?

ju-mun-ha-si-ge-sseo-yo?

Can I order now?

지금 주문해도 돼요?

ji-geum ju-mun-hae-do dwae-yo?

What would you like?

뭘 주문하시겠습니까?

mwol ju-mun-ha-si-get-sseum-ni-gga?

We'd like to order drinks first.

먼저 음료부터 시킬게요.

meon-jeo eum-nyo-bu-teo si-kil-gge-yo

We are ready to order.

주문하고 싶은데요.

ju-mun-ha-go si-peun-de-yo

I'd like this one, please.

이것으로 주세요.

i-geo-seu-ro ju-se-yo

Okay, I'll have that.

좋아요, 그걸로 할게요.

jo-a-yo, geu-geol-ro hal-gge-yo

The same for me, please.

저도 같은 것으로 주세요.

jeo-do ga-teun geo-seu-ro ju-se-yo

Let me check your order.

주문 확인하겠습니다.

ju-mun hwa-gin-ha-get-sseum-ni-da

Anything else?

더 필요하신 것 없으세요?

deo pi-ryo-ha-sin geot eop-sseu-se-yo?

Which options would you like for your jeukseok tteokbokki?

즉석 떡볶이에 어떤 사리를 하시겠어요?

jeuk-sseok ddeok-bbo-ggi-e eo-ddeon sa-ri-reul
ha-si-ge-sseo-yo?

Please add a coil of ramyeon and a coil of chewy noodles.

라면사리 하나, 쫄면사리 하나 추가해
주세요.

ra-myeon-sa-ri ha-na, jjol-myeon-sa-ri ha-na chu-ga-hae
ju-se-yo

I'd like a cheese gimbap and a tuna gimbap.

치즈김밥 하나, 참치김밥 하나 주세요.

chi-jeu-gim-bbap ha-na, cham-chi-gim-bbap ha-na ju-se-yo

Which one do you want, mul-naengmyeon or bibim-naengmyeon?

물냉면으로 드릴까요 비빔냉면으로 드릴까요?

mul-raeng-myeo-neu-ro deu-ril-gga-yo

bi-bim-naeng-myeo-neu-ro deu-ril-gga-yo?

You can enjoy a cup of insam-ju if you order a samgye-tang.

삼계탕을 시키면 인삼주가 서비스로 나옵니다.

sam-gye-tang-eul si-ki-myeon in-sam-ju-ga seo-bi-seu-ro na-om-ni-da

Please keep the bibimbap and red pepper paste separate.

비빔밥에 고추장을 따로 주세요.

bi-bim-bba-be go-chu-jang-eul dda-ro ju-se-yo

I'd like a sundubu-jjigae.

순두부찌개 하나 주세요.

sun-du-bu-jji-gae ha-na ju-se-yo

Don't put a spring onion into seolleong-tang.

설렁탕에 파를 넣지 마세요.

seol-reong-tang-e pa-reul neo-chi ma-se-yo

Pork bellies for three, please.

삼겹살 3인분 주세요.

sam-gyeop-ssal sa-min-bun ju-se-yo

Sundae for two, please. And put the livers on the side.

순대 2인분 주세요. 간도 주세요.

sun-dae i-in-bun ju-se-yo. gan-do ju-se-yo

Beverages

What would you like to drink?

어떤 음료로 하시겠어요?

eo-ddeon eum-nyo-ro ha-si-ge-sseo-yo?

A bottle of soju.

소주 한 병 주세요.

so-ju han byeong ju-se-yo

Water is self-servise.

물은 셀프입니다.

mu-reun sel-peu-im-ni-da

Water's fine with me.

물이면 됩니다.

mu-ri-myeon doem-ni-da

Just coffee, please.

커피만 주세요.

keo-pi-man ju-se-yo

I'd like a daechu-cha.

대추차 주세요.

dae-chu-cha ju-se-yo

Special Requests

Don't add salt, please.

소금을 넣지 마세요.

so-geu-meul neo-chi ma-se-yo

Don't add red pepper paste, please.

고추장을 넣지 마세요.

go-chu-jang-eul neo-chi ma-se-yo

Don't make it too spicy, please.

너무 맵게 하지 마세요.

neo-mu maep-gge ha-ji ma-se-yo

Can I have more rice?

밥 좀 더 주세요.

bap jom deo ju-se-yo

Please refill the side dishes.

반찬 더 주세요.

ban-chan deo ju-se-yo

Server Q&A

\# What are the ingredients for this?

이 음식의 재료는 뭐예요?

i eum-si-ge jae-ryo-neun mwo-ye-yo?

\# How is it cooked?

이것은 어떻게 한 거죠?

i-geo-seun eo-ddeo-ke han geo-jyo?

\# I dropped my chopsticks.

젓가락을 떨어뜨렸어요.

jeot-gga-ra-geul ddeo-reo-ddeu-ryeo-sseo-yo

\# Could you clean the table, please?

테이블 좀 치워 주세요.

te-i-beul jom chi-wo ju-se-yo

Do you have any dishes without meat? I'm vegetarian.

고기가 안 들어간 음식 있어요?
저는 채식주의자거든요.

go-gi-ga an deu-reo-gan eum-sik i-sseo-yo?
jeo-neun chae-sik-jju-i-ja-geo-deun-yo

Complaints

\# My order hasn't come yet.

주문한 요리가 아직 안 나왔어(요).

ju-mun-han yo-ri-ga a-jik an na-wa-sseo(-yo)

\# This is not what I ordered.

이건 제가 주문한 요리가 아닌데요.

i-geon je-ga ju-mun-han yo-ri-ga a-nin-de-yo

\# I'm afraid this meat is not done enough.

고기가 완전히 익지 않았어(요).

go-gi-ga wan-jeon-hi ik-jji a-na-sseo(-yo)

There's something strange in it.

여기에 뭔가 이상한 게 들어 있어(요).

yeo-gi-e mwon-ga i-sang-han ge deu-reo i-sseo(-yo)

It tastes a little strange.

맛이 좀 이상한데(요).

ma-si jom i-sang-han-de(-yo)

I'm afraid this bread is stale.

이 빵은 상한 것 같은데(요).

i bbang-eun sang-han geot ga-teun-de(-yo)

Personal Tastes

Did you enjoy your meal?

식사는 어떠셨어요?

sik-ssa-neun eo-ddeo-syeo-sseo-yo?

It's the best meal I've ever had.

이렇게 맛있는 음식은 처음 먹어봤어(요).

i-reo-ke ma-din-neun eum-si-geun cheo-eum
meo-geo-bwa-sseo(-yo)

It's a little too sweet for me.

좀 달았어(요).

jom da-ra-sseo(-yo)

It's a little salty.

맛이 좀 짰어(요).

ma-si jom jja-sseo(-yo)

It's a little spicy.

좀 매웠어(요).

jom mae-wo-sseo(-yo)

Sorry, but it's not really my taste.

죄송하지만, 제 입맛에 맞지 않아요.

joe-song-ha-ji-man, je im-ma-se mat-jji a-na-yo

Paying the Bill

Check, please.

계산서 주세요.

gye-san-seo ju-se-yo

Where is the cashier?

어디에서 계산하나요?

eo-di-e-seo gye-san-ha-na-yo?

Let's go Dutch for lunch.

점심은 각자 내자.

jeom-si-meun gak-jja nae-ja

점심은 더치페이하자.

jeom-si-meun deo-chi-pe-i-ha-ja

I'll treat you today.

오늘 내가 한턱낼게(요).

o-neul nae-ga han-teong-nael-gge(-yo)

오늘 내가 쏠게(요).

o-neul nae-ga ssol-gge(-yo)

How much in all?

다 얼마예요?

da eol-ma-ye-yo?

The total comes to 54,000 won.

총 5만 4천 원입니다.

chong o-man sa-cheon won-im-ni-da

Will you pay in cash or by credit card?

현금으로 하시겠어요 신용카드로
하시겠어요?

hyeon-geu-meu-ro ha-si-ge-sseo-yo si-nyong-ka-deu-ro
ha-si-ge-sseo-yo?

By credit card, please.

카드로 할게요.

ka-deu-ro hal-gge-yo

Can I pay by credit card?

신용카드로 해도 돼요?

si-nyong-ka-deu-ro hae-do dwae-yo?

I'd like to pay in cash.

현금으로 할게요.

hyeon-geu-meu-ro hal-gge-yo

Here is your change.

거스름돈입니다.

geo-seu-reum-ddo-nim-ni-da

잔돈입니다.

jan-do-nim-ni-da

Can I have a receipt, please?

영수증 주세요.

yeong-su-jeung ju-se-yo

Here is your receipt.

영수증입니다.

yeong-su-jeung-im-ni-da

Coffee

Shall we have a cup of iced coffee?

함께 아이스커피 할래(요)?

ham-gge a-i-seu-keo-pi hal-rae(-yo)?

Let's talk over a cup of coffee.

우리 커피 마시면서 얘기해(요).

u-ri keo-pi ma-si-myeon-seo yae-gi-hae(-yo)

I'd like an espresso.

에스프레소 주세요.

e-seu-peu-re-so ju-se-yo

I'll have a decaf latte, please.

디카페인 카페라테 주세요.

di-ka-pe-in ka-pe-ra-te ju-se-yo

Would you like some sugar or cream in your coffee?

커피에 설탕과 크림을 넣으세요?

keo-pi-e seol-tang-gwa keu-ri-meul neo-eu-se-yo?

Hold the whipped cream on the caffè mocha.

카페모카에 휘핑크림은 빼 주세요.

ka-pe-mo-ka-e hwi-ping-keu-ri-meun bbae ju-se-yo

Fast Food

Next in line, please.

다음 손님, 주문하세요.

da-eum son-nim, ju-mun-ha-se-yo

186

With no mayo.

마요네즈를 넣지 마세요.

ma-yo-ne-jeu-reul neo-chi ma-se-yo

For here or to go?

여기에서 드실 건가요 가져가실 건가요?

yeo-gi-e-seo deu-sil ggeon-ga-yo ga-jeo-ga-sil ggeon-ga-yo?

Does the burger come with cheese?

햄버거 안에 치즈가 있나요?

haem-beo-geo a-ne chi-jeu-ga in-na-yo?

The set includes a beverage and French fries.

세트에 음료수와 감자튀김이 포함됩니다.

se-teu-e eum-nyo-su-wa gam-ja-twi-gi-mi
po-ham-doem-ni-da

We'll have that ready in a minute.

1분 안에 다 됩니다.

il-bun a-ne da doem-ni-da

Food Delivery

Let's get some pizza!

우리 피자 시켜 먹자!

u-ri pi-ja si-kyeo meok-jja!

I'd like to order two jjajangmyeon, one jjambbong and tangsuyuk.

짜장면 둘, 짬뽕 하나, 탕수육 하나
시킬게요.

jja-jang-myeon dul, jjam-bbong ha-na, tang-su-yuk ha-na
si-kil-gge-yo

Do you deliver to Han-il apartment?

한일아파트로 배달되나요?

ha-nil-a-pa-teu-ro bae-dal-doe-na-yo?

How soon will the pizza get here?

피자 배달하는 데 얼마나 걸려요?

pi-ja bae-dal-ha-neun de eol-ma-na geol-ryeo-yo?

Can you deliver it in 30 minutes or less?

30분 내에 배달되나요?

sam-sip-bbun nae-e bae-dal-doe-na-yo?

Going Shopping

\# I'm a shopaholic.

난 쇼핑광이에요.

nan syo-ping-gwang-i-e-yo

\# You really like luxury goods, don't you?

넌 명품만 밝히는구나, 그렇지?

neon myoeng-pum-man bal-ki-neun-gu-na, geu-reo-chi?

\# I'm an impulsive shopper.

나는 충동구매자예요.

na-neun chung-dong-gu-mae-ja-ye-yo

\# What time does the Mega Mall open?

메가몰은 몇 시에 열어(요)?

me-ga-mo-reun myeot si-e yeo-reo(-yo)?

\# What time does the Mega Mall close?

메가몰은 몇 시에 닫아(요)?

me-ga-mo-reun myeot si-e da-da(-yo)?

Why don't we go shopping together?

같이 쇼핑하러 가지 않을래(요)?

ga-chi syo-ping-ha-reo ga-ji a-neul-rae(-yo)?

I like hanging out with my friends in the shopping mall.

난 친구들과 쇼핑센터에서 돌아다니기를 좋아해(요).

nan chin-gu-deul-gwa syo-ping-sen-teo-e-seo do-ra-da-ni-gi-reul jo-a-hae(-yo)

We went shopping for gifts.

우리는 선물을 사려고 쇼핑했어(요).

u-ri-neun seon-mu-reul sa-ryeo-go syo-ping-hae-sseo(-yo)

This neighborhood is great for shopping.

이 근처는 쇼핑하기 아주 좋아(요).

i geun-cheo-neun syo-ping-ha-gi a-ju jo-a(-yo)

We do our shopping at midnight.

우리는 심야에 쇼핑해(요).

u-ri-neun si-mya-e syo-ping-hae(-yo)

It's convenient to buy something online.
온라인 쇼핑이 편리해(요).

ol-ra-in syo-ping-i pyeol-ri-hae(-yo)

Clothing Shops

May I help you?
뭘 도와드릴까요?

mwol do-wa-deu-ril-gga-yo?

I'm just looking around.
그냥 좀 둘러볼게요.

geu-nyang jom dul-reo-bol-gge-yo

What styles are popular now?
요즘 어떤 스타일이 유행하죠?

yo-jeum eo-ddeon seu-ta-i-ri yu-haeng-ha-jyo?

This seems to be out of fashion.
이건 이미 유행이 지난 것 같은데(요).

i-geon i-mi yu-haeng-i ji-nan geot ga-teun-de(-yo)

Can I try this on?

한번 입어 봐도 될까요?

han-beon i-beo bwa-do doel-gga-yo?

Where is the fitting room?

탈의실이 어디예요?

ta-ri-si-ri eo-di-ye-yo?

What size do you wear?

사이즈가 어떻게 되세요?

sa-i-jeu-ga eo-ddeo-ke doe-se-yo?

Mediums don't fit me. I think I need a large.

미디엄 사이즈는 맞지 않아요. 라지 사이즈를
입어야 할 거 같아요.

mi-di-eom sa-i-jeu-neun mat-jji a-na-yo. ra-ji sa-i-jeu-reul
i-beo-ya hal ggeo ga-ta-yo

Does it come in a larger size?

더 큰 사이즈 있어요?

deo keun sa-i-jeu i-sseo-yo?

Do you have other styles?

다른 스타일 있어요?

da-reun seu-ta-il i-sseo-yo?

Do you have other colors?

다른 색 있어요?

da-reun saek i-sseo-yo?

Do you have this in red?

이거 빨간색 있어요?

i-geo bbal-gan-saek i-sseo-yo?

That looks great on you!

정말 어울리네!

jeong-mal eo-ul-ri-ne!

너한테 딱인데!

neo-han-te dda-gin-de!

Which one is the dress that the mannequin is wearing?

저 마네킹이 입은 원피스는 어떤 거죠?

jeo ma-ne-king-i i-beun won-pi-seu-neun eo-ddeon geo-jyo?

This is just what I'm looking for.

이것은 바로 제가 찾던 거예요.

i-geo-seun ba-ro je-ga chat-ddeon geo-ye-yo

You should go with that one.

저 옷을 사는 게 좋겠어(요).

jeo o-seul sa-neun ge jo-ke-sseo(-yo)

I'll look around at a few more places and then decide.

몇 군데 더 돌아보고 결정하자.

myeot gun-de deo do-ra-bo-go gyeol-jjeong-ha-ja

The Mall

Where can I find the electric appliances?

전자제품은 어디에 있어요?

jeon-ja-je-pu-meun eo-di-e i-sseo-yo?

Is the supermarket in the basement?

슈퍼마켓은 지하에 있어요?

syu-peo-ma-ke-seun ji-ha-e i-sseo-yo?

I think we better get a shopping cart.

쇼핑 카트를 가져오는 게 낫겠어(요).

syo-ping ka-teu-reul ga-jeo-o-neun ge nat-gge-sseo(-yo)

Can you break up the set?

낱개 판매하나요?

nat-ggae pan-mae-ha-na-yo?

Can I taste it?

시식해도 돼요?

si-si-kae-do dwae-yo?

Do you have this in stock?

이거 재고 있어요?

i-geo jae-go i-sseo-yo?

Sales & Discounts

Are you currently having a sale?

지금 할인하고 있어요?

ji-geum ha-rin-ha-go i-sseo-yo?

When is it going to be on sale?

언제 할인해요?

eon-je ha-rin-hae-yo?

When does the sale end?

할인은 언제 끝나요?

ha-ri-neun eon-je ggeun-na-yo?

The sale ended yesterday.

할인은 어제 끝났어요.

ha-ri-neun eo-je ggeun-na-sseo-yo

The summer sales are on now.

지금은 여름 할인합니다.

ji-geu-meun yeo-reum ha-rin-ham-ni-da

We are having a clearance sale.

재고 정리 할인 중입니다.

jae-go jeong-ri ha-rin jung-im-ni-da

The winter sale will go on for a week.

겨울 할인이 일주일 동안 계속됩니다.

gyeo-ul ha-ri-ni il-jju-il dong-an gye-sok-doem-ni-da

Do you know when this item will go on sale again?

이 상품은 언제 또 할인해요?

i sang-pu meun eon-je ddo ha-rin-hae-yo?

Which items are on sale?

어떤 상품들이 할인하고 있어요?

eo-ddeon sang-pum-deu-ri ha-rin-ha-go i-sseo-yo?

Sale prices are good through May 31st.

이 할인 가격은 5월 31일까지입니다.

i ha-rin ga-gyeo-geun o-wol sam-si-bi-il-gga-ji-im-ni-da

The spring sale starts this Friday.

봄 할인은 이번 주 금요일부터 시작합니다.

bom ha-ri-neun i-beon ju geu-myo-il-bu-teo si-ja-kam-ni-da

The sale is from December 20th to the 31st.

할인은 12월 20일부터 31일까지입니다.

ha-ri-neun si-bi-wol i-si-bil-bu-teo
sam-si-bi-ril-gga-ji-im-ni-da

Everything's 20% off.

전 상품은 20퍼센트 할인합니다.

jeon sang-pu-meun i-sip-peo-sen-teu ha-rin-ham-ni-da

There's a 25% off sale today.

오늘은 25퍼센트 할인합니다.

o-neu-reun i-si-bo-peo-sen-teu ha-rin-ham-ni-da

It's regularly priced at 80,000 won but it's on sale for 64,000 won.

정가는 8만 원인데, 할인해서
6만 4천 원입니다.

jeong-gga-neun pal-man wo-nin-de, ha-rin-hae-seo
yung-man sa-cheon wo-nim-ni-da

Buy one, get the second half-price.

한 벌 사시면, 다른 한 벌은 50퍼센트
할인해 드려요.

han beol sa-si-myeon, da-reun han beo-reun
o-sip-peo-sen-teu ha-rin-hae deu-ryeo-yo

T-shirts are on sale. Buy 3 shirts and get the 4th free.

티셔츠가 할인 중입니다. 세 벌 사시면,
한 벌 드립니다.

ti-syeo-cheu-ga ha-rin jung-im-ni-da. se beol sa-si-myeon,
han beol deu-rim-ni-da

On Installment

Can I buy it on an installment plan?

할부로 살 수 있어요?

hal-bu-ro sal ssu i-sseo-yo?

Would you like to pay in full or in installments?

일시불이에요 할부예요?

il-ssi-bu-ri-e-yo hal-bu-ye-yo?

How many installments would you like to make?

몇 개월 할부로 하시겠어요?

myeot gae-wol hal-bu-ro ha-si-ge-sseo-yo?

I'd like to make three no-interest payments.

3개월 무이자 할부로 할게요.

sam-gae-wol mu-i-ja hal-bu-ro hal-gge-yo

If you put 50% down, we'll sell it in installments.

계약금으로 50퍼센트를 내시면, 잔금을 할부로 해 드립니다.

gye-yak-ggeu-meu-ro o-sip-peo-sen-teu-reul nae-si-myeon,
jan-geu-meul hal-bu-ro hae deu-rim-ni-da

How much do I pay per month?

한 달에 얼마씩 내나요?

han da-re eol-ma-ssik nae-na-yo?

Delivery

Could you deliver them to my house?

집까지 배송해 줄 수 있어요?

jip-gga-ji bae-song-hae jul ssu i-sseo-yo?

Does the price include the delivery charge?

배송비가 포함된 가격인가요?

bae-song-bi-ga po-ham-doen ga-gyeo-gin-ga-yo?

It's free delivery for all purchases over 50,000 won.

5만 원 이상 구입하면 무료 배송입니다.

o-man won i-sang gu-i-pa-myeon mu-ryo bae-song-im-ni-da

If I purchase it now, can I get it today?

지금 구입하면, 오늘 받을 수 있어요?

ji-geum gu-i-pa-myeon, o-neul ba-deul ssu i-sseo-yo?

When will it be delivered?

언제 배달해 주세요?

eon-je bae-dal-hae ju-se-yo?

We can deliver overnight.

구매한 다음 날 보내 드립니다.

gu-mae-han da-eum nal bo-nae deu-rim-ni-da

Refunds & Exchanges

I'd like to get a refund for this.

반품해 주세요.

ban-pum-hae ju-se-yo

When should I return this by?

언제까지 반품해야 해요?

eon-je-gga-ji ban-pum-hae-ya hae-yo?

Within 2 weeks from the day you bought it.

구매일로부터 2주 내입니다.

gu-mae-il-ro-bu-teo i-ju nae-im-ni-da

You can't return it without the receipt.

영수증이 없으면, 반품이 안 됩니다.

yeong-su-jeung-i eop-sseu-myeon, ban-pu-mi an
doem-ni-da

No refund, no return.

환불 및 반품 불가.

hwan-bul mit ban-pum bul-ga

We're not allowed to make exchanges or give refunds for items bought on sale.

할인 기간에 구입한 물건은 교환이나 환불이 안 됩니다.

ha-rin gi-gan-e gu-i-pan mul-geo-neun gyo-hwa-ni-na
hwan-bu-ri an doem-ni-da

Appointments

\# Where is the reception desk, please?

접수처가 어디예요?

jeop-ssu-cheo-ga eo-di-ye-yo?

\# I'd like to make an appointment to see the doctor.

진찰을 예약하고 싶은데요.

jin-cha-reul ye-ya-ka-go si-peun-de-yo

\# Have you ever visited here before?

저희 병원에 처음 오신 건가요?

jeo-hi byeong-wo-ne cheo-eum o-sin geon-ga-yo?

\# Today is my first visit.

오늘이 처음인데요.

o-neu-ri cheo-eu-min-de-yo

I'd like to get a physical exam.

건강검진을 받고 싶은데요.

geon-gang-geom-ji-neul bat-ggo si-peun-de-yo

What are your office hours?

진료 시간이 어떻게 됩니까?

jil-ryo si-ga-ni eo-ddeo-ke doem-ni-gga?

I have an appointment to see Dr. Jeong at 1 o'clock.

1시에 정 선생님께 진료 예약을 했어요.

han-si-e jeong seon-saeng-nim-gge jil-ryo ye-ya-geul hae-sseo-yo

Does Dr. Kim have office hours on Tuesdays?

김 선생님 화요일에도 진료하시나요?

gim seon-saeng-nim hwa-yo-i-re-do jil-ryo-ha-si-na-yo?

Until what time do you give consultations today?

오늘 몇 시까지 진료해요?

o-neul myeot si-gga-ji jil-ryo-hae-yo?

I don't have an appointment. Can I still get in?

예약을 하지 않았는데요. 진찰받을 수 있나요?

ye-ya-geul ha-ji a-nan-neun-de-yo. jin-chal-ba-deul ssu in-na-yo?

The doctor is booked up today.

오늘 진료 예약은 마감됐습니다.

o-neul jil-ryo ye-ya-geun ma-gam-dwaet-sseum-ni-da

Medical Treatments

What's the matter?

어디가 불편하세요?

eo-di-ga bul-pyeon-ha-se-yo?

어디가 안 좋으세요?

eo-di-ga an jo-eu-se-yo?

What are your symptoms?

어떤 증상이 있으세요?

eo-ddeon jeung-sang-i i-sseu-se-yo?

Have you ever suffered from this before?

전에 이 병을 앓은 적 있으세요?

jeo-ne i byeong-eul a-reun jeok i-sseu-se-yo?

Let's take your temperature.

체온을 좀 재 보겠습니다.

che-o-neul jom jae bo-get-sseum-ni-da

Take a deep breath.

심호흡하세요.

sim-ho-heu-pa-se-yo

Would you please lift up your shirt? I'll examine you.

셔츠를 걷어 보세요. 진찰하겠습니다.

syeo-cheu-reul geo-deo bo-se-yo.
jin-chal-ha-get-sseum-ni-da

Surgery

I have a swollen foot.

발이 부었어요.

ba-ri bu-eo-sseo-yo

I broke my leg in a car accident.

교통사고로 다리가 부러졌어요.

gyo-tong-sa-go-ro da-ri-ga bu-reo-jeo-sseo-yo

I fell down and skinned my knees.

넘어져서 무릎이 까졌어요.

neo-meo-jeo-seo mu-reu-pi gga-jeo-sseo-yo

I have a backache.

허리가 아파요.

heo-ri-ga a-pa-yo

I sprained my ankle.

발목이 삐었어요.

bal-mo-gi bbi-eo-sseo-yo

My shoulders are stiff.

어깨가 결려요.

eo-ggae-ga gyeol-ryeo-yo

When can my cast come off?

깁스는 언제 풀 수 있어요?

gip-sseu-neun eon-je pul ssu i-sseo-yo?

I cut my finger with a knife.

칼에 손가락을 베었어요.

ka-re son-gga-ra-geul be-eo-sseo-yo

I'm black and blue all over.

온몸에 멍이 들었어요.

on-mo-me meong-i deu-reo-sseo-yo

I had an appendectomy.

지난주에 맹장수술을 했어요.

ji-nan-ju-e maeng-jang-su-su-reul hae-sseo-yo

This is a simple operation. Don't worry.

이것은 간단한 수술이에요. 걱정하지 마세요.

i-geo-seun gan-dan-han su-su-ri-e-yo. geok-jjeong-ha-ji
ma-se-yo

I had metal pins inserted into the fractured leg.

골절된 다리에 철심을 박았어요.

gol-jjeol-doen da-ri-e cheol-ssi-meul ba-ga-sseo-yo

Internal Medicine - Colds

\# I seem to have caught a cold.

감기에 걸린 것 같아요.

gam-gi-e geol-rin geot ga-ta-yo

\# I have a stuffy nose.

코가 막혔어요.

ko-ga ma-kyeo-sseo-yo

\# I have a runny nose.

콧물이 나요.

kon-mu-ri na-yo

\# I had a persistent cough for over a month.

한 달 이상 기침감기를 앓았어요.

han dal i-sang gi-chim-gam-gi-reul a-ra-sseo-yo

\# My throat hurts when I swallow.

침을 삼킬 때마다 목이 아파요.

chi-meul sam-kil ddae-ma-da mo-gi a-pa-yo

There's a lot of flu going around.
독감이 유행하고 있어요.

dok-gga-mi yu-haeng-ha-go i-sseo-yo

Internal Medicine - Fevers

I have a fever.
열이 나요.

yeo-ri na-yo

I have a temperature of 39 degrees.
열이 39도까지 나요.

yeo-ri sam-sip-ggu-do-gga-ji na-yo

I have a terrible headache.
머리가 깨질 듯 아파요.

meo-ri-ga ggae-jil ddeut a-pa-yo

The fever hasn't left me.
열이 내리지 않아요.

yeo-ri nae-ri-ji a-na-yo

I have a fever and my whole body aches.

열이 나고 온몸이 아파요.

yeo-ri na-go on-mo-mi a-pa-yo

Did you take a fever reducer?

해열제 먹었어요?

hae-yeol-jje meo-geo-sseo-yo?

I have a fever and my throat is sore.

열도 나고 목도 아파요.

yeol-do na-go mok-ddo a-pa-yo

Internal Medicine - Digestive System

My stomach is upset.

배가 아파요.

bae-ga a-pa-yo

I have a pain in my abdomen.

아랫배가 아파요.

a-raet-bbae-ga a-pa-yo

I am having trouble with my stomach.

속이 안 좋아요.

so-gi an jo-a-yo

I think I have food poisoning.

식중독에 걸린 거 같아요.

sik-jjung-do-ge geol-rin geo ga-ta-yo

I feel like vomiting.

구역질이 나요.

gu-yeok-jji-ri na-yo

I throw up when I eat.

먹으면 토해요.

meo-geu-myeon to-hae-yo

I've got the runs.

배탈이 났어요.

bae-ta-ri na-sseo-yo

I'm constipated.

변비예요.

byeon-bi-ye-yo

I've had no bowel movement for a few days.

요즘 며칠 계속 변을 못 봤어요.

yo-jeum myeo-chil gye-sok byeo-neul mot bwa-sseo-yo

I've had diarrhea since yesterday.

어제부터 설사했어요.

eo-je-bu-teo seol-ssa-hae-sseo-yo

I've had diarrhea all day long since yesterday.

어제 종일 설사했어요.

eo-je jong-il seol-ssa-hae-sseo-yo

I am suffering from chronic indigestion.

만성 소화불량을 겪고 있어요.

man-seong so-hwa-bul-ryang-eul gyeok-ggo i-sseo-yo

Dental Clinic - Toothaches

I have a severe toothache.

이가 몹시 아파요.

i-ga mop-ssi a-pa-yo

This back tooth hurts me.

어금니가 아파요.

eo-geum-ni-ga a-pa-yo

I have a minor toothache.

치통이 약간 있어요.

chi-tong-i yak-ggan i-sseo-yo

I have a toothache whenever I eat. I can't eat anything.

먹으면 이가 아파서요. 아무것도 못 먹어요.

meo-geu-myeon i-ga a-pa-seo-yo. a-mu-geot-ddo mot meo-geo-yo

I can't chew on this side of my mouth.

치통 때문에 이쪽으로 씹을 수 없어요.

chi-tong ddae-mu-ne i-jjo-geu-ro ssi-beul ssu eop-sseo-yo

Dental Clinic

I have a loose tooth.

이 하나가 흔들려요.

i ha-na-ga heun-deul-ryeo-yo

This tooth should be taken out.

이를 빼야 할 것 같아요.

i-reul bbae-ya hal ggeot ga-ta-yo

How much is a filling?

이를 때우는 데 얼마예요?

i-reul ddae-u-neun de eol-ma-ye-yo?

You'd rather not have your wisdom tooth extracted yet.

아직 사랑니를 뽑지 않는 것이 좋겠어요.

a-jik sa-rang-ni-reul bbop-jji an-neun geo-si jo-ke-sseo-yo

My gums bleed whenever I floss.

치실을 쓸 때마다 잇몸에서 피가 나요.

chi-si-reul sseul ddae-ma-da in-mo-me-seo pi-ga na-yo

When will I get my braces off?

언제 치아 교정기를 빼요?

eon-je chi-a-gyo-jeong-gi-reul bbae-yo?

I think I have a cavity.

충치가 생긴 것 같아요.

chung-chi-ga saeng-gin geot ga-ta-yo

It looks like you have two small cavities.

충치 두 개가 있는데, 심하지는 않아요.

chung-chi du gae-ga in-neun-de, sim-ha-ji-neun a-na-yo

I need to have my cavity filled in.

이 충치는 때워야겠어요.

i chung-chi-neun ddae-wo-ya-ge-sseo-yo

I want to bleach my teeth.

치아 미백을 받고 싶어요.

chi-a mi-bae-geul bat-ggo si-peo-yo

Can you recommend a good dentist?

좋은 치과 의사 선생님을 추천해 줄 수
있어(요)?

jo-eun chi-gwa ui-sa seon-saeng-ni-meul chu-cheon-hae
jul ssu i-sseo(-yo)?

Other Treatments

I'm allergic to pollen.

꽃가루에 알레르기가 있어요.

ggot-gga-ru-e al-re-reu-gi-ga i-sseo-yo

I suffer from anemia.

빈혈이 있어요.

bin-hyeo-ri i-sseo-yo

I often get nose bleeds.

코피가 자주 나요.

ko-pi-ga ja-ju na-yo

I have high blood pressure.

고혈압이 있어요.

go-hyeo-ra-bi i-sseo-yo

I've got a strange rash.

두드러기가 났어요.

du-deu-reo-gi-ga na-sseo-yo

I have an asthma attack.

천식 발작이 있어요.

cheon-sik bal-jja-gi i-sseo-yo

I've got eczema on my hand.

손에 습진이 생겼어요.

so-ne seup-jji-ni saeng-gyeo-sseo-yo

I missed a mothly period.

생리를 건너뛰었어요.

saeng-ri-reul geon-neo-ddwi-eo-sseo-yo

Hospitalization

I've come to be admitted.

입원 수속을 하려고 합니다.

i-bwon su-so-geul ha-ryeo-go ham-ni-da

Do I have to stay here overnight?

입원해야 하나요?

i-bwon-hae-ya ha-na-yo?

You should be admitted right away.

바로 입원 수속하세요.

ba-ro i-bwon su-so-ka-se-yo

How long will I have to be in the hospital?

얼마나 입원해야 하나요?

eol-ma-na i-bwon-hae-ya ha-na-yo?

Will my insurance policy cover my stay here?

입원하면 의료보험이 적용되나요?

i-bwon-ha-myeon ui-ryo-bo-heo-mi jeo-gyong-doe-na-yo?

I would like to have a private room if possible.

가능하면 1인실로 해 주세요.

ga-neung-ha-myeon i-rin-sil-ro hae ju-se-yo

Operations

The patient is seriously ill.

지금 환자의 상태기 위급합니다.

ji-geum hwan-ja-e sang-tae-ga wi-geu-pam-ni-da

I'm afraid he may not see this month out.

아마 이 달을 넘기지 못할 겁니다.

a-ma i da-reul neom-gi-ji mo-tal ggeom-ni-da

Do I need surgery? / Do I need an operation?

수술해야 하나요?

su-sul-hae-ya ha-na-yo?

Have you ever had any operations?

수술한 적 있어요?

su-sul-han jeok i-sseo-yo?

I had a C-section.

제왕절개 수술을 했습니다.

je-wang-jeol-gae su-su-reul haet-sseum-ni-da

What's the recovery time?

회복 기간은 어떻게 돼요?

hoe-gok gi-ga-neun eo-ddeo-ke dwae-yo?

Medical Costs & Insurance

How much will it be for this visit?

진찰비가 얼마예요?

jin-chal-bi-ga eol-ma-ye-yo?

Do you have health insurance?

건강보험 있어요?

geon-gang-bo-heom i-sseo-yo?

I don't have health insurance.

건강보험에 가입하지 않았어요.

geon-gang-bo-heo-me ga-i-pa-ji a-na-sseo-yo

Does my insurance cover all the costs?

모든 비용은 보험 적용이 돼요?

mo-deun bi-yong-eun bo-heom jeo-gyong-i dwae-yo?

Some kinds of medicine are not covered by insurance.

일부 의약품은 보험 적용이 안 됩니다.

il-bu ui-yak-pu-meun bo-heom jeo-gyong-i an doem-ni-da

It covers only half of the costs.

반액만 보험 적용이 됩니다.

ba-naeng-man bo-heom jeo-gyong-i doem-ni-da

Visiting the Sick

Please take good care of yourself!

몸조심 해(요)!

mom-jo-sim hae(-yo)!

I hope you will get well soon.

속히 회복되길 바랍니다.

so-ki hoe-bok-ddoe-gil ba-ram-ni-da

Good luck!

건강하세요!

geon-gang-ha-se-yo!

I'm sorry to hear you've been sick.
편찮으시다니 유감입니다.

pyeon-cha-neu-si-da-ni yu-ga-mim-ni-da

I hope it's nothing serious.
병이 심각하지 않기를 바라(요).

byeong-i sim-ga-ka-ji an-ki-reul ba-ra(-yo)

I'm glad you're feeling better!
회복되셨다니, 다행입니다!

hoe-bok-ddoe-syeot-dda-ni, da-haeng-im-ni-da!

Prescriptions

I'll prescribe some medicine.
처방전을 써 드릴게요.

cheo-bang-jeo-neul sseo deu-ril-gge-yo

I'll prescribe some medicine for 3 days.
3일치 처방전을 드릴게요.

sa-mil-chi cheo-bang-jeo-neul deu-ril-gge-yo

225

Are you taking any medication?

현재 복용하는 약이 있어요?

hyeon-jae bo-gyong-ha-neun ya-gi i-sseo-yo?

Are you allergic to any medicine?

알레르기 있는 약 있어요?

al-re-reu-gi in-neun yak i-sseo-yo?

It will make you feel a little drowsy.

이 약은 먹으면 졸릴 수 있습니다.

i ya-geun meo-geu-myeon jol-ril ssu it-sseum-ni-da

Does this medicine have any side effects?

이 약은 어떤 부작용이 있습니까?

i ya-geun eo-ddeon bu-ja-gyong-i it-sseum-ni-gga?

The Pharmacy

Can I get this prescription filled?

이 처방전대로 조제해 주세요.

i cheo-bang-jeon-dae-ro jo-je-hae ju-se-yo

You can't buy this without a prescription.

처방전이 없으면 약을 살 수 없습니다.

cheo-bang-jeo-ni eop-sseu-myeon ya-geul sal ssu
eop-sseum-ni-da

May I have some sleeping pills?

수면제 좀 주세요.

su-myeon-je jom ju-se-yo

Do you have any pain-killers?

진통제 있어요?

jin-tong-je i-sseo-yo?

Ointment, please.

연고 주세요.

yeon-go ju-se-yo

How should I take this medicine?

이 약은 어떻게 먹죠?

i ya-geun eo-ddeo-ke meok-jjyo?

How many should I take per day?

하루에 몇 알씩 먹어요?

ha-ru-e myeot al-ssik meo-geo-yo?

Take one every 4 hours.

4시간마다 한 알씩 먹어요.

ne si-gan-ma-da han al-ssik meo-geo-yo

Take this medicine one capsule at a time.

이 약은 한 번에 한 알씩 먹어요.

i ya-geun han beo-ne han al-ssik meo-geo-yo

Three times a day before meals.

하루에 세 번, 식사 전에 먹습니다.

ha-ru-e se beon, sik-ssa jeo-ne meok-sseum-ni-da

Could you recommend a supplement to strengthen immunity?

면역력을 강화하는 영양제 추천해 주세요.

myeo-nyeong-nyeo-geul gang-hwa-ha-neun yeong-yang-je
chu-cheon-hae ju-se-yo

The Bank

\# Please take a number.

번호표를 뽑으세요.

beon-ho-pyo-reul bbo-beu-se-yo

\# I'd like to open a bank account.

계좌를 개설하려고 하는데요.

gye-jwa-reul gae-seol-ha-ryeo-go ha-neun-de-yo

\# What type of account do you want?

어떤 종류의 예금을 하시겠습니까?

eo-ddeon jong-nyu-e ye-geu-meul ha-si-get-sseum-ni-gga?

\# I want to start Internet banking.

인터넷뱅킹을 신청하고 싶은데요.

in-teo-net-baeng-king-eul sin-cheong-ha-go si-peun-de-yo

\# Would you like to apply for a debit card, too?

체크카드도 만드실 건가요?

che-keu-ka-deu-do man-deu-sil ggeon-ga-yo?

Could you endorse this check, please?

이 수표에 이서해 주시겠어요?

i su-pyo-e i-seo-hae ju-si-ge-sseo-yo?

A savings account or a checking account?

저축 예금인가요 아니면 당좌 예금인가요?

jeo-chuk ye-geu-min-ga-yo a-ni-myeon dang-jwa
ye-geu-min-ga-yo? ·

What's the interest rate?

이율은 얼마죠?

i-yu-reun eol-ma-jyo?

I'd like to close my bank account.

계좌를 해지하려고요.

gye-jwa-reul hae-ji-ha-ryeo-go-yo

I'd like to check my transactions for last
month.

제 계좌의 거래 내역을 확인하고 싶어요.

je gye-jwa-e geo-rae nae-yeo-geul hwa-gin-ha-go si-peo-yo

Could you break this (into smaller bills)?

잔돈으로 교환할 수 있어요?

jan-do-neu-ro gyo-hwan-hal ssu i-sseo-yo?

I'd like to get an e-passbook.

전자통장으로 바꾸고 싶어요.

jeon-ja-tong-jang-eu-ro ba-ggu-go si-peo-yo

Deposits & Withdrawals

How much do you want to deposit today?

오늘 얼마를 예금하시겠어요?

o-neul eol-ma-reul ye-geum-ha-si-ge-sseo-yo?

I'd like to make a deposit of 1,000,000 won..

100만 원을 예금하려고요.

baeng-man wo-neul ye-geum-ha-ryeo-go-yo

How much do you want to withdraw?

얼마를 인출하실 거예요?

eol-ma-reul in-chul-ha-sil ggeo-ye-yo?

I want to withdraw 300,000 won.

30만 원을 인출하려는데요.

sam-sim-man wo-neul in-chul-ha-ryeo-neun-de-yo

I'd like to set up an automatic withdrawal for my electric bill.

전기요금을 자동이체로 지정해 주세요.

jeon-gi-yo-geu-meul ja-dong-i-che-ro ji-jeong-hae ju-se-yo

Remittances

Please transfer the funds to this account.

이 계좌로 송금해 주세요.

i gye-jwa-ro song-geum-hae ju-se-yo

We need your bank's name and address, your bank account number and the bank routing number.

은행 이름과 주소, 계좌번호와 송금번호를 알려 주세요.

eun-haeng i-reum-gwa ju-so, gye-jwa-beon-ho-wa song-geum-beon-ho-reul al-ryeo ju-se-yo

I'd like to make a remittance to the U.S.

미국으로 송금하려고 합니다.

mi-gu-geu-ro song-geum-ha-ryeo-go ham-ni-da

Is there a bank fee for transferring money? How much?

송금 수수료가 있어요? 얼마예요?

song-geum su-su-ryo-ga i-sseo-yo? eol-ma-ye-yo?

There's an 800 won charge.

수수료는 800원입니다.

su-su-ryo-neun pal-bae-gwo-nim-ni-da

ATMs

Where are the ATMs?

ATM은 어디에 있어요?

e-i-ti-e-meun eo-di-e i-sseo-yo?

How do I make a deposit?

어떻게 입금해요?

eo-ddeo-ke ip-ggeum-hae-yo?

Please insert your card here.

카드를 여기에 넣으세요.

ka-deu-reul yeo-gi-e neo-eu-se-yo

Please enter your PIN number.

비밀번호를 누르세요.

bi-mil-beon-ho-reul nu-reu-se-yo

Please press the account balance key.

잔액조회 버튼을 누르세요.

ja-naek-jjo-hoe beo-teu-neul nu-reu-se-yo

The ATM ate my card.

ATM이 카드를 먹어 버렸어요.

e-i-ti-e-mi ka-deu-reul meo-geo beo-ryeo-sseo-yo

Credit Cards

When will my card be issued?

신용카드가 언제 발급되나요?

si-nyong-ka-deu-ga eon-je bal-geup-ddoe-na-yo?

What is the expiry date of this credit card?

이 카드의 유효기간은 언제까지예요?

i ka-deu-e yu-hyo-gi-ga-neun eon-je-gga-ji-ye-yo?

How much is the limit for this card?

사용 한도액이 어떻게 되나요?

sa-yong han-do-ae-gi eo-ddeo-ke doe-na-yo?

I want to check my latest credit card statement.

최근 신용카드 사용내역을 확인하고 싶은데요.

choe-geun si-nyong-ka-deu sa-yong-nae-yeo-geul hwa-gin-ha-go si-peun-de-yo

I had my credit card stolen. Please cancel it.

신용카드를 도난당했어요. 해지해 주세요.

si-nyong-ka-deu-reul do-nan-dang-hae-sseo-yo. hae-ji-hae ju-se-yo

Exchanges

\# Do you exchange foreign currency?

환전할 수 있어요?

hwan-jeon-hal ssu i-sseo-yo?

\# I'd like to exchange U.S. dollars for Korean won.

달러를 원화로 바꾸고 싶어요.

dal-reo-reul won-hwa-ro ba-ggu-go si-peo-yo

\# How would you like your bills?

어떻게 환전해 드릴까요?

eo-ddeo-ke hwan-jeon-hae deu-ril-gga-yo?

\# Please give it to me in 10,000 won bills.

전액 만 원짜리로 주세요.

jeo-naek man won-jja-ri-ro ju-se-yo

We get a 2% commission of the exchanged amount.

환전 비용의 2%를 수수료로 받습니다.

hwan-jeon bi-yong-e i-peo-sen-teu-reul su-su-ryo-ro
bat-sseum-ni-da

There is a change booth across the street.

길 건너편에 환전소가 있습니다.

gil geon-neo-pyeo-ne hwan-jeon-so-ga it-sseum-ni-da

Exchange Rates

What's today's rate for Korean won?

오늘 원화의 환율은 얼마예요?

o-neul won-hwa-e hwa-nyu-reun eol-ma-ye-yo?

Today's exchange rate is 92 cents U.S. to 1,000 won.

오늘 환율은 천 원에 0.92달러입니다.

o-neul hwa-nyu-reun cheon wo-ne
yeong-jjeom-gu-i-dal-reo-im-ni-da

What's the rate for Korean won to Euros?

원화를 유로로 환전하는 환율이 어떻게
돼요?

won-hwa-reul yu-ro-ro hwan-jeon-ha-neun hwa-nyu-ri
eo-ddeo-ke dwae-yo?

Has the won risen against the pound?

파운드에 대한 원 환율이 올랐어요?

pa-un-deu-e dae-han won hwa-nyu-ri ol-ra-sseo-yo?

Should I exchange some money now?

지금 환전해야 할까요?

ji-geum hwan-jeon-hae-ya hal-gga-yo?

Loans

Can foreigners get loans at this bank?

외국인이 이 은행에서 대출할 수 있어요?

oe-gu-gi-ni i eun-haeng-e-seo dae-chul-hal ssu i-sseo-yo?

I'd like to discuss a bank loan.

대출 문제로 상담하고 싶은데요.

dae-chul mun-je-ro sang-dam-ha-go si-peun-de-yo

Has my loan been approved?

제 대출이 승인되었나요?

je dae-chu-ri seung-in-doe-eon-na-yo?

I'm going to take out a loan to pay my tuition.

학자금 대출을 신청하고 싶은데요.

hak-jja-geum dae-chu-reul sin-cheong-ha-go si-peun-de-yo

I put my house up as collateral for the loan.

집을 담보로 대출을 받았어요.

ji-beul dam-bo-ro dae-chu-reul ba-da-sseo-yo

I got a loan at 4% interest.

4부 이자로 대출을 받았어요.

sa-bu i-ja-ro dae-chu-reul ba-da-sseo-yo

Sending Letters

\# How much is the postage for this letter?

이 편지 요금은 얼마예요?

i pyeon-ji yo-geu-meun eol-ma-ye-yo?

\# By express or regular mail?

빠른우편인가요 보통우편인가요?

bba-reu-nu-pyeo-nin-ga-yo bo-tong-u-pyeo-nin-ga-yo?

\# How much is it to send this letter by express mail?

빠른우편으로 보내는 데 얼마인가요?

bba-reu-nu-pyeo-neu-ro bo-nae-neun de eol-ma-in-ga-yo?

\# Please register this letter.

등기우편으로 해 주세요.

deun-ggi-u-pyeo-neu-ro hae ju-se-yo

\# By airmail or surface mail?

항공편인가요 배편인가요?

hang-gong-pyeo-nin-ga-yo bae-pyeo-nin-ga-yo?

Could I have three 330 won stamps?

330원짜리 우표 세 장 주세요.

sam-baek-ssam-si-bwon-jja-ri u-pyo se jang ju-se-yo

What is the zip code?

우편번호가 뭐예요?

u-pyeon-beon-ho-ga mwo-ye-yo?

Postage will be paid by the addressee.

우편 요금은 착불입니다.

u-pyeon yo-geu-meun chak-bbu-rim-ni-da

How long does it take to reach Seoul?

서울까지 가는 데 얼마나 걸려요?

seo-ul-gga-ji ga-neun de eol-ma-na geol-ryeo-yo?

It will take 3 days to get there.

사흘 후에 도착합니다.

sa-heul hu-e do-cha-kam-ni-da

Where do I write the addressee's name and address?

수신인의 이름과 주소를 어디에 쓰면 돼요?

su-si-ni-ne i-reum-gwa ju-so-reul eo-di-e sseu-myeon dwae-yo?

I want to send this letter to Daegu.

이 편지를 대구로 보내려고요.

i pyeon-ji-reul dae-gu-ro bo-nae-ryeo-go-yo

Packages

Would you weigh this parcel?

소포 무게를 달아주세요.

so-po mu-ge-reul da-ra-ju-se-yo

Please wrap this parcel in package paper.

이 소포를 포장해 주세요.

i so-po-reul po-jang-hae ju-se-yo

242

What does your parcel contain?

소포 안에는 뭐죠?

so-po a-ne-neun mwo-jyo?

Please be careful, this parcel is fragile.

조심해 주세요, 깨지기 쉬운 물건입니다.

jo-sim-hae ju-se-yo, ggae-ji-gi swi-un mul-geo-nim-ni-da

Please insure this parcel just in case.

만일을 대비해 소포를 보험에 가입해 주세요.

ma-ni-reul dae-bi-hae so-po-reul bo-heo-me ga-i-pae
ju-se-yo

The Hair Salon

\# I need a new hair style.

새로운 헤어스타일을 하고 싶어요.

sae-ro-un he-eo-seu-ta-i-reul ha-go si-peo-yo

\# How would you like your hair?

어떤 헤어스타일을 원하세요?

eo-ddeon he-eo-seu-ta-i-reul won-ha-se-yo?

\# May I show you a hair style book?

헤어스타일 책을 보여 드릴까요?

he-eo-seu-ta-il chae-geul bo-yeo deu-ril-gga-yo?

\# Could you recommend something for me?

좀 추천해 주시겠어요?

jom chu-cheon-hae ju-si-ge-sseo-yo?

\# I want to look like the model in this photo.

이 사진의 모델 헤어스타일을 하고 싶어요.

i sa-ji-e mo-del he-eo-seu-ta-i-reul ha-go si-peo-yo

I'll leave it up to you.

알아서 어울리게 해 주세요.

a-ra-seo eo-ul-ri-ge hae ju-se-yo

Haircuts

I need to get my hair cut.

커트하려고요.

keo-teu-ha-ryeo-go-yo

How do you want it cut?

어떻게 잘라 드릴까요?

eo-ddeo-ke jal-ra deu-ril-gga-yo?

Leave it this long, please.

이 정도 자르려고요.

i jeong-do ja-reu-ryeo-go-yo

Can you cut it shoulder length?

어깨 길이로 잘라 주세요.

eo-ggae gi-ri-ro jal-ra ju-se-yo

I'd like to have my hair cut short.

머리를 짧게 자르고 싶어요.

meo-ri-reul jjal-gge ja-reu-go si-peo-yo

Please take a few inches off the ends.

머리끝을 살짝 다듬어 주세요.

meo-ri-ggeu-teul sal-jjak da-deu-meo ju-se-yo

I want a crew cut.

스포츠형으로 잘라 주세요.

seu-po-cheu-hyeong-eu-ro jal-ra ju-se-yo

I'd like bobbed hair.

단발머리를 하고 싶어요.

dan-bal-meo-ri-reul ha-go si-peo-yo

I'd like to have bangs, too.

앞머리도 잘라 주세요.

am-meo-ri-do jal-ra ju-se-yo

I'd like to keep my bangs.

앞머리는 그대로 두세요.

am-meo-ri-neun geu-dae-ro du-se-yo

I want my hair layered.

머리에 층을 내 주세요.

meo-ri-e cheung-eul nae ju-se-yo

Don't cut it too short.

너무 짧게 자르지 마세요.

neo-mu jjal-gge ja-reu-ji ma-se-yo

Perms

I want to get a perm.

파마하려고요.

pa-ma-ha-ryeo-go-yo

What kind of perm do you want?

어떤 스타일로 파마하시겠어요?

eo-ddeon seu-ta-il-ro pa-ma-ha-si-ge-sseo-yo?

I'd like my hair wavy.

웨이브 파마로 해 주세요.

we-i-beu pa-ma-ro hae ju-se-yo

I want to get rid of my curls.

스트레이트 파마로 해 주세요.

seu-teu-re-i-teu pa-ma-ro hae ju-se-yo

Don't curl my hair too much, please.

너무 곱슬거리지 않게 해 주세요.

neo-mu gop-sseul-geo-ri-ji an-ke hae ju-se-yo

Your perm came out nicely.

파마가 잘 나왔네요.

pa-ma-ga jal na-wan-ne-yo

Coloring

I'd like to have my hair dyed, please.

염색하려고요.

yeom-sae-ka-ryeo-go-yo

What color do you want your hair dyed?

어떤 색으로 염색하시겠어요?

eo-ddeon sae-geu-ro yeom-sae-ka-si-ge-sseo-yo?

Can you color my hair brown?

갈색으로 염색해 주세요.

gal-ssae-geu-ro yeom-sae-kae ju-se-yo

Highlighting makes you look younger.

밝게 염색하면 어려 보여요.

bal-gge yeom-sae-ka-myeon eo-ryeo bo-yeo-yo

Can you hide the gray hair with coloring?

흰머리를 염색해 주세요.

hin-meo-ri-reul yeom-sae-kae ju-se-yo

Your hair has been seriously damaged by too much coloring.

염색을 자주 해서 머릿결이 심하게 손상됐어요.

yeom-sae-geul ja-ju hae-seo meo-rit-ggyeo-ri sim-ha-ge son-sang-dwae-sseo-yo

Putting in the Laundry

\# I'm going to take these clothes to the cleaner's.

이 옷은 내가 세탁소에 맡길게요.

i o-seun nae-ga se-tak-sso-e mat-ggil-gge-yo

\# Can you put this suit in at the laundry?

이 양복을 세탁소에 맡겨 주세요.

i yang-bo-geul se-tak-sso-e mat-ggyeo ju-se-yo

\# I'd like these pants to be pressed.

이 바지를 다려 주세요.

i ba-ji-reul da-ryeo ju-se-yo

\# Could I get this cardigan dry cleaned?

이 카디건을 드라이클리닝 해 주세요.

i ka-di-geo-neul deu-ra-i-keul-ri-ning hae ju-se-yo

I'll need this suit cleaned by next Monday.

다음 주 월요일까지 세탁해 주세요.

da-eum ju wo-ryo-il-gga-ji se-ta-kae ju-se-yo

Collecting the Laundry

When can I get it back?

언제 찾을 수 있어요?

eon-je cha-jeul ssu i-sseo-yo?

I want to pick up my laundry.

옷 찾으러 왔어요.

ot cha-jeu-reo wa-sseo-yo

Is my laundry ready?

제 옷은 세탁이 다 됐나요?

je o-seun se-ta-gi da dwaen-na-yo?

Here's my claim ticket.

여기 세탁물 보관증입니다.

yeo-gi se-tang-mul bo-gwan-jjeung-im-ni-da

What's the charge for cleaning?

세탁비는 얼마예요?

se-tak-bbi-neun eol-ma-ye-yo?

How much do you charge to dry-clean this coat?

이 코트 드라이클리닝 비용은 얼마예요?

i ko-teu deu-ra-i-keul-ri-ning bi-yong-eun eol-ma-ye-yo?

Getting Stains Out

Can you get this stain out?

얼룩을 제거해 주세요.

eol-ru-geul je-geo-hae ju-se-yo

Could you take out the stains on these pants?

이 바지의 얼룩을 제거해 주세요.

i ba-ji-e eol-ru-geul je-geo-hae ju-se-yo

I spilled coffee all over my skirt.

커피를 치마에 쏟았어요.

keo-pi-reul chi-ma-e sso-da-sseo-yo

The dry cleaner can remove the stain.

드라이클리닝을 하면 얼룩을 지울 수 있어요.

deu-ra-i-keul-ri-ning-eul ha-myeon eol-ru-geul ji-ul ssu i-sseo-yo

This stain won't wash out.

이 얼룩은 빨아서 지워지지 않아요.

i eol-ru-geun bba-ra-seo ji-wo-ji-ji a-na-yo

The stain didn't come out.

얼룩이 제대로 빠지지 않았어요.

eol-ru-gi je-dae-ro bba-ji-ji a-na-sseo-yo

Mending

Do you fix clothes?

옷을 수선할 수 있나요?

o-seul su-seon-hal ssu in-na-yo?

Could you mend this jacket?

이 재킷을 좀 수선해 주세요.

i jae-ki-seul jom su-seon-hae ju-se-yo

I'd like to have these pants shortened.

이 바지를 좀 줄여 주세요.

i ba-ji-reul jom ju-ryeo ju-se-yo

Could you lengthen these pants?

이 바지 기장을 좀 늘여 주세요.

i ba-ji gi-jang-eul jom neu-ryeo ju-se-yo

I'm sorry I can't fix that.

죄송하지만, 수선할 수 없어요.

joe-song-ha-ji-man, su-seon-hal ssu eop-sseo-yo

This zipper fell off. Can you replace it?

지퍼가 떨어졌어요. 좀 고쳐 주세요.

ji-peo-ga ddeo-reo-jeo-sseo-yo. jom go-cheo ju-se-yo

Rental Cars

Can I rent a car this Saturday?

이번 주 토요일에 차를 빌리려고요.

i-beon ju to-yo-i-re cha-reul bil-ri-ryeo-go-yo

Can I pick up a rental car at the airport?

공항에서 렌터카를 받을 수 있어요?

gong-hang-e-seo ren-teo-ka-reul ba-deul ssu i-sseo-yo?

What kind of car do you want?

어떤 차를 빌리시겠어요?

eo-ddeon cha-reul bil-ri-si-ge-sseo-yo?

I want a compact car.

소형차를 빌리려고 합니다.

so-hyeong-cha-reul bil-ri-ryeo-go ham-ni-da

How long will you need it?

얼마나 빌리실 겁니까?

eol-ma-na bil-ri-sil ggeom-ni-gga?

I'd like to rent a car for 5 days.

5일 동안 빌리려고요.

o-il dong-an bil-ri-ryeo-go-yo

What's your rental fee?

렌탈 요금은 얼마입니까?

ren-tal yo-geu-meun eol-ma-im-ni-gga?

65,000 won per day.

하루에 6만 5천 원입니다.

ha-ru-e yung-man o-cheon wo-nim-ni-da

Do you want insurance?

보험에 가입하시겠어요?

bo-heo-me ga-i-pa-si-ge-sseo-yo?

With full coverage, please.

종합 보험에 가입해 주세요.

jong-hap bo-heo-me ga-i-pae ju-se-yo

Where should I leave the car?

차를 어디로 반납하나요?

cha-reul eo-di-ro ban-na-pa-na-yo?

You can return the car to any branch in the country.

전국 지점 어느 곳으로나 반납이 가능합니다.

jeon-guk ji-jeom eo-neu go-seu-ro-na ban-na-bi
ga-neung-ham-ni-da

Gas Stations

Is there a gas station around here?

이 근처에 주유소가 있어(요)?

i geun-cheo-e ju-yu-so-ga i-sseo(-yo)?

Let's pull up to that gas station.

주유소에 들릅시다.

ju-yu-so-e deul-reup-ssi-da

Can you direct me to the nearest gas station?

가장 가까운 주유소는 어디예요?

ga-jang ga-gga-un ju-yu-so-neun eo-di-ye-yo?

Do you have enough gas?

기름이 충분해(요)?

gi-reu-mi chung-bun-hae(-yo)?

We're running low on gas.

기름이 떨어져 가는데(요).

gi-reu-mi ddeo-reo-jeo ga-neun-de(-yo)

Pull over at the next gas station.

다음 주유소에서 차를 세워(요).

da-eum ju-yu-so-e-seo cha-reul se-wo(-yo)

I need some gas.

기름을 넣어야 해(요).

gi-reu-meul neo-eo-ya hae(-yo)

The tank is almost empty.

기름이 거의 떨어졌어(요).

gi-reu-mi geo-i ddeo-reo-jeo-sseo(-yo)

This is a self-service gas station.

이 주유소는 셀프 주유입니다.

i ju-yu-so-neun sel-peu ju-yu-im-ni-da

Do I have to pump the gas myself?

내가 직접 주유해야 하나요?

nae-ga jik-jjeop ju-yu-hae-ya ha-na-yo?

Fill it up, please.

기름 가득 넣어 주세요.

gi-reum ga-deuk neo-eo ju-se-yo

Fill it up with regular gas, please.

일반 휘발유요, 가득 넣어 주세요.

il-ban hwi-bal-ryu-yo, ga-deuk neo-eo ju-se-yo

Give me 50,000 worth, please.

5만 원어치 넣어 주세요.

o-mam wo-neo-chi neo-eo ju-se-yo

Washing & Servicing Cars

Wash it down, please.

세차해 주세요.

se-cha-hae ju-se-yo

Could you wash and wax the car?

세차하고, 왁스를 발라 주세요.

se-cha-ha-go, wak-sseu-reul bal-ra ju-se-yo

How much is it to wash the car?

세차하는 데 얼마예요?

se-cha-ha-neun de eol-ma-ye-yo?

Check the oil, please.

엔진오일 좀 봐 주세요.

en-ji-no-il jom bwa ju-se-yo

Check the windshield wipers, please.

앞 유리 와이퍼 좀 점검해 주세요.

ap yu-ri wa-i-peo jom jeom-geom-hae ju-se-yo

Is there enough washer fluid?

워셔액이 충분한가요?

wo-syeo-ae-gi chung-bun-han-ga-yo?

Would you check my tires?

타이어 좀 점검해 주세요.

ta-i-eo jom jeom-geom-hae ju-se-yo

The Bookstore

\# This bookstore has a large number of books
for children.

이 서점에는 아동 도서가 많이 있어(요).

i seo-joe-me-nuen a-dong do-seo-ga ma-ni i-sseo(-yo)

\# That bookstore specializes in computer
books.

저 서점은 컴퓨터 서적을 전문적으로
취급해(요).

jeo seo-jeo-meun keom-pyu-teo seo-jeo-geul
jeon-mun-jjeo-geu-ro chwi-geu-pae(-yo)

\# You can buy that book anywhere.

그 책은 어디서나 살 수 있어(요).

geu chae-geun eo-di-seo-na sal ssu i-sseo(-yo)

There's a good secondhand bookstore not far from here.

근처에 괜찮은 헌책방이 있어(요).

geun-cheo-e gwaen-cha-neun heon-chaek-bbang-i i-sseo(-yo)

근처에 괜찮은 중고 서점이 있어(요).

geun-cheo-e gwaen-cha-neun jung-go seo-jeo-mi i-sseo(-yo)

This is my favorite bookstore.

여기는 내 단골 책방이에요.

yeo-gi-neun nae dan-gol chaek-bbang-i-e-yo

Searching for Books

Excuse me, do you have <Toji>?

실례지만, 〈토지〉라는 책이 있나요?

sil-rye-ji-man, <to-ji>-ra-neun chae-gi in-na-yo?

Where are the books on history?

역사에 관한 책은 어디 있죠?

yeok-ssa-e gwan-han chae-geun eo-di it-jjyo?

Do you know who wrote <The Great Gatsby>?

〈위대한 개츠비〉 누가 썼는지 알아(요)?

<wi-dae-han gae-cheu-bi> nu-ga sseon-neun-ji a-ra(-yo)?

Do you have a foreign language section?

외국어 코너 있어요?

oe-gu-geo ko-neo i-sseo-yo?

What's the title of the book?

책 제목이 뭐예요?

chaek je-mo-gi mwo-ye-yo?

I can't find the book I'm looking for.

제가 사려는 책을 찾을 수 없어요.

je-ga sa-ryeo-neun chae-geul cha-jeul ssu eop-sseo-yo

I'm calling to see if you have any copies of <Korean Grammar> left.

〈한국어 문법〉 책이 있는지 물어보려고 전화했어요.

<han-gu-geo mun-bbeop> chae-gi in-neun-ji
mu-reo-bo-ryeo-go jeon-hwa-hae-sseo-yo

When will the book come out?

그 책은 언제 나옵니까?

geu chae-geun eon-je na-om-ni-gga?

The book will be put on sale soon.

그 책은 곧 판매됩니다.

geu chae-geun got pan-mae-doem-ni-da

The book came out in September.

이 책은 9월에 출간됐어요.

i chae-geun gu-wo-re chul-gan-dwae-sseo-yo

The book is out of print.

이 책은 절판됐습니다.

i chae-geun jeol-pan-dwaet-sseum-ni-da

Could you give me the title of the book you want?

원하는 책 제목을 알려 주시겠어요?

won-ha-neun chaek je-mo-geul al-ryeo ju-si-ge-sseo-yo?

Books Online

If I ordered it today, when would I get it?

오늘 주문하면, 언제 받을 수 있어요?

o-neul ju-mun-ha-myeon, eon-je ba-deul ssu i-sseo-yo?

Are the books on online much cheaper?

인터넷 서점에서 사는 책은 많이 싸(요)?

in-teo-net seo-jeo-me-seo sa-neun chae-geun ma-ni ssa(-yo)?

What's the current bestseller?

요즘 베스트셀러는 뭐예요?

yo-jeum be-seu-teu-sel-reo-neun mwo-ye-yo?

Why don't you buy it online?

인터넷 서점에서 사는 게 어때(요)?

in-teo-net seo-jeo-me-seo sa-neun ge eo-ddae(-yo)?

They sell paper books and e-books.

종이책과 이북을 팔고 있어(요).

jong-i-chaek-ggwa i-bu-geul pal-go i-sseo(-yo)

Paying for Books

I bought <The Korean Cookbook> for 18,000 won.

〈한국 요리책〉을 만 8천 원에 샀어(요).

<han-guk yo-ri-chae>-geul man pal-cheon wo-ne sa-sseo(-yo)

The book will cost somewhere around 10,000 won.

그 책은 아마 만 원쯤 할 걸(요).

geu chae-geun a-ma man won-jjeum hal ggeol(-yo)

The regular price is 20,000 won but you get a 10% discount.

원래 2만 원인데, 권 당 10% 할인해 드립니다.

wol-rae i-man wo-nin-de, gwon dang sip-peo-sen-teu ha-rin-hae deu-rim-ni-da

We will exchange the book if there's any problem.

파본은 교환해 드립니다.

pa bo neun gyo-hwan-hae deu-rim-ni-da

I bought the books on impulse as they were so cheap.

책이 싸길래 충동구매 해 버렸어(요).

chae-gi ssa-gil-rae chung-dong-gu-mae hae beo-ryeo-sseo(-yo)

The Library

The book I want isn't in the library.

제가 필요한 책이 도서관에 없어요.

je-ga pi-ryo-han chae-gi do-seo-gwa-ne eop-sseo-yo

You should be quiet in the library.

도서관에서는 조용히 해야 해(요).

do-seo-gwa-ne-seo-neun jo-yong-hi hae-ya hae(-yo)

Don't use a cell phone in the library.

도서관에서는 휴대폰을 사용하면 안 돼(요).

do-seo-gwa-ne-seo-neun hyu-dae-po-neul
sa-yong-ha-myeon an dwae(-yo)

This library has a collection of 30,000 volumes.

이 도서관은 3만 권의 책을 소장하고 있어(요).

i do-seo-gwa-neun sam-man gwo-ne chae-geul
so-jang-ha-go i-sseo(-yo)

I'd like to get a library card.

도서관 카드를 만들려고요.

do-seo-gwan ka-deu-reul man-deul-ryeo-go-yo

He is borrowing books from the library.

그는 도서관에서 책을 빌리고 있어(요).

geu-neun do-seo-gwa-ne-seo chae-geul bil-ri-go i-sseo(-yo)

We were reading books in the library.

우리는 도서관에서 책을 읽고 있었어(요).

u-ri-neun do-seo-gwa-ne-seo chae-geul il-ggo
i-sseo-sseo(-yo)

Where can I find the magazines?

잡지가 어디에 있어(요)?

jap-jji-ga eo-di-e i-sseo(-yo)?

Is there a photocopier I can use?

복사기를 쓸 수 있어요?

bok-ssa-gi-reul sseul ssu i-sseo-yo?

The library is going to close in a half hour.

도서관은 30분 후에 문을 닫아(요).

do-seo-gwa-neun sam-sip-bbun hu-e mu-neul da-da(-yo)

Checking Out Books

How many books can I borrow at one time?

한 번에 몇 권 빌릴 수 있어요?

han beo-ne myeot gwon bil-ril ssu i-sseo-yo?

I'd like to explain about checking out and returning books.

대출과 반납에 관련된 규정을 설명해 드릴게요.

dae-chul-gwa ban-na-be gwal-ryeon-doen gyu-jeong-eul seol-myeong-hae deu-ril-gge-yo

The check-out limit is 5 books.

다섯 권까지 대출할 수 있습니다.

da-seot gwon-gga-ji dae-chul-hal ssu it-sseum-ni-da

I'd like to check out 4 books.

네 권을 대출하려고요.

ne gwo-neul dae-chul-ha-ryeo-go-yo

How can I check out a book?

대출하려면 어떻게 해야 하죠?

dae-chul-ha-ryeo-myeon eo-ddeo-ke hae-ya ha-jyo?

I forgot my card. Can I still check out a book?

제 카드를 깜박했는데요. 그래도 책을
대출할 수 있어요?

je ka-deu-reul ggam-ba-kaen-neun-de-yo. geu-rae-do
chae-geul dae-chul-hal ssu i-sseo-yo?

Returning Books

The library books need to be returned by
tomorrow.

도서관 책은 내일까지 반납해야 해(요).

do-seo-gwan chae-geun nae-il-gga-ji ban-na-pae-ya hae(-yo)

\# I have to go to the library to return some books due today.

오늘까지 반납해야 하는 책이 있어서, 도서관에 가야 해(요).

o-neul-gga-ji ban-na-pae-ya ha-neun chae-gi i-sseo-seo, do-seo-gwa-ne ga-ya hae(-yo)

\# This book has been checked out to next Monday.

이 책은 다음 주 월요일까지 대출되어 있습니다.

i chae-geun da-eum ju wo-ryo-il-gga-ji dae-chul-doe-eo it-sseum-ni-da

\# What happens if I lose a book?

책을 잃어버리면 어떻게 돼죠?

chae-geul i-reo-beo-ri-myeon eo-ddeo-ke dwae-jyo?

\# Could I renew this book?

이 책을 연장할 수 있어요?

i chae-geul yeon-jang-hal ssu i-sseo-yo?

Church

\# I go to church on Sundays.

일요일마다 교회에 가(요).

i-ryo-il-ma-da gyo-hoe-e ga(-yo)

\# I always attend a Sunday worship service.

주일 예배는 꼭 참석해(요).

ju-il ye-bae-neun ggok cham-seo-kae(-yo)

\# Is there anything different about a Korean service?

한국어 예배에는 뭐 다른 게 있어(요)?

han-gu-geo ye-bae-e-neun mwo da-reun ge i-sseo(-yo)?

\# What was the topic of today's sermon?

오늘 설교의 주제가 뭐예요?

o-neul seol-gyo-e ju-je-ga mwo-ye-yo?

What scripture is today's sermon based on?

오늘 예배의 성경 구절은 뭐예요?

o-neul ye-bae-e seong-gyeong gu-jeo-reun mwo-ye-yo?

Turn to the Gospel according to John, chapter 3, verse 16.

요한복음 3장 16절을 펴세요.

yo-han-bo-geum sam-jang sim-nyuk-jjeo-reul pyeo-se-yo

The pastor's sermon was touching today.

오늘 목사님의 설교는 감동적이었어(요).

o-neul mok-ssa-ni-me seol-gyo-neun
gam-dong-jeo-gi-eo-sseo(-yo)

The sermon was so long that I got sleepy.

설교가 길어서 졸렸어(요).

seol-gyo-ga gi-reo-seo jol-ryeo-sseo(-yo)

I don't have any money for the collection.

돈이 없어서 헌금을 못 냈어(요).

do-ni eop-sseo-seo heon-geu-meul mot nae-sseo(-yo)

How long have you attended this church?

이 교회를 얼마나 다녔어(요)?

i gyo-hoe-reul eol-ma-na da-nyeo-sseo(-yo)?

Christmas and Easter are important church festivals.

성탄절과 부활절은 교회의 큰 행사예요.

seong-tan-jeol-gwa bu-hwal-jjeo-reun gyo-hoe-e keun haeng-sa-ye-yo

She sings in the church choir.

그녀는 교회 성가대에서 노래해(요).

geu-nyeo-neun gyo-hoe seong-ga-dae-e-seo no-rae-hae(-yo)

Let us kneel in prayer.

무릎 꿇고 기도합시다.

mu-reup ggul-ko gi-do-hap-ssi-da

I pray in Jesus' name. Amen.

예수님의 이름으로 기도합니다. 아멘.

ye-su-ni-me i-reu-meu-ro gi-do-ham-ni-da. a-men

My prayer was answered.

기도가 응답되었어(요).

gi-do-ga eung-dap-ddoe-eo-sseo(-yo)

Do you mind if I say a prayer before eating?

식사 전에 기도해도 될까요?

sik-ssa jeo-ne gi-do-hae-do doel-gga-yo?

We give thanks to God before this meal.

우리는 식사 전에 감사 기도해(요).

u-ri-neun sik-ssa jeo-ne gam-sa gi-do-hae(-yo)

Cathedrals

Myeong-jin prayed the rosary.

명진이는 묵주 기도를 했어(요).

myeong-ji-ni-neun muk-jju gi-do-reul hae-sseo(-yo)

I made my cross and prayed.

십자가를 그리고 기도했어(요).

sip-jja-ga-reul geu-ri-go gi-do-hae-sseo(-yo)

The Father celebrated Mass.

신부님은 미사를 올렸어(요).

sin-bu-ni-meun mi-sa-reul ol-ryeo-sseo(-yo)

The memorial mass will be held at the catholic cathedaral tomorrow 5 p.m.

추모 미사는 내일 오후 5시에 성당에서 드립니다.

chu-mo mi-sa-neun nae-il o-hu da-seot-ssi-e
seong-dang-e-seo deu-rim-ni-da

He has come to give his confession.

그는 고해성사를 하러 왔어(요).

geu-neun go-hae-seong-sa-reul ha-reo wa-sseo(-yo)

I confessed to the priest.

신부님께 고해성사를 했어(요).

sin-bu-nim-gge go-hae-seong-sa-reul hae-sseo(-yo)

Temples

\# My grandmother goes to a temple to worship.

할머니는 불공드리러 절에 가셔(요).

hal-meo-ni-neun bul-gong-deu-ri-reo jeo-re ga-syeo(-yo)

\# Where should I do a temple stay?

템플스테이 하러 어디로 가야 할까요?

tem-peul-seu-te-i ha-reo eo-di-ro ga-ya hal-gga-yo?

\# I feel soothed whenever I go to the temple.

그 절에 가면 마음이 안정돼(요).

geu jeo-re ga-myeon ma-eu-mi an-jeong-dwae(-yo)

\# Can we meet a Buddhist monk here?

여기에서 스님을 뵐 수 있을까요?

yeo-gi-e-seo seu-ni-meul boel ssu i-sseul-gga-yo?

When the monk sounds a wooden gong, everyone bows to Buddha.

스님이 목탁을 두드리면, 모두 부처님께 절을 합니다.

seu-ni-mi mok-ta-geul du-deu-ri-myeon, mo-du bu-cheo-nim-gge jeo-reul ham-ni-da

Mosques

Do you know any Korean Muslims?

한국 무슬림 알아(요)?

han-guk mu-seul-rim a-ra(-yo)?

Muslims visit mosques to pray.

무슬림들은 기도하기 위해 모스크에 가(요).

mu-seul-rim-deu-reun gi-do-ha-gi wi-hae mo-seu-keu-e ga(-yo)

The masjid or mosque is the place of Muslim worship.

회교 사원이나 모스크는 무슬림의 예배처예요.

hoe-gyo sa-wo-ni-na mo-seu-keu-neun mu-seul-ri-me ye-bae-cheo-ye-yo

There is a mosque in Itaewon. Do you know any others?

이태원에 모스크가 있잖아(요). 다른 곳 알아(요)?

i-tae-wo-ne mo-seu-keu-ga it-jja-na(-yo). da-reun got a-ra(-yo)?

What should I wear to the mosque?

모스크에 들어갈 때는 어떻게 입어야 해(요)?

mo-seu-keu-e deu-reo-gal ddae-neun eo-ddeo-ke i-beo-ya hae(-yo)?

Movie Theaters

\# I'll meet you in front of the theater at 6:30!

6시 반에 극장 입구에서 만나(요)!

yeo-seot-ssi ba-ne geuk-jjang ip-ggu-e-seo man-na(-yo)!

\# Which theater do you want to go to?

어느 극장으로 갈 거예요?

eo-neu geuk-jjang-eu-ro gal ggeo-ye-yo?

\# That movie is showing at the CC theater.

저 영화는 CC극장에서 상영해(요).

jeo yeong-hwa-neun ssi-ssi-geuk-jjang-e-seo
sang-yeong-hae(-yo)

\# Where do you like to sit?

어떤 좌석으로 드릴까요?

eo-ddeon jwa-seo-geu-ro deu-ril-gga-yo?

I'd like to sit in the front row.

앞쪽 좌석으로 주세요.

ap-jjok jwa-seo-geu-ro ju-se-yo

I can't see very well. Do you want to move?

잘 안 보여(요). 옮길래(요)?

jal an bo-yeo(-yo). om-gil-rae(-yo)?

There are many multiplex theaters in Korea.

한국에는 복합 영화 상영관이 많이 있어(요).

han-gu-ge-neun bo-kap yeong-hwa sang-yeong-gwa-ni
ma-ni i-sseo(-yo)

Did you book tickets for the 3D theater?

3D 상영관으로 예매했어(요)?

sseu-ri-di sang-yeong-gwa-neu-ro ye-mae-hae-sseo(-yo)?

At 4D theaters, audiences can experience the wind blowing, see chairs moving, or smell certain odors during key moments in the film.

4D 상영관에서는 주요 장면에서 바람이 불거나 의자가 움직이거나 냄새가 나(요).

po-di sang-yeong-gwa-ne-seo-neun ju-yo jang-myeo-ne-seo ba-ra-mi bul-geo-na ui-ja-ga um-ji-gi-geo-na naem-sae-ga na(-yo)

I got to the theater too late to see the beginning.

극장에 너무 늦게 도착해서, 영화를 처음부터 못 봤어(요).

geuk-jjang-e neo-mu neut-gge do-cha-kae-seo, yeong-hwa-reul cheo-eum-bu-teo mot bwa-sseo(-yo)

Movie Tickets

It's getting late. We should probably get our tickets.

늦겠어(요). 우리 표를 사 둬야 할 걸(요).

neut-gge-sseo(-yo). u-ri pyo-reul sa dwo-ya hal ggeol(-yo)

You can't get a refund now. The movie's already started.

지금은 환불할 수 없어(요). 영화가 이미 시작했거든(요).

ji-geu-meun hwan-bul-hal ssu eop-sseo(-yo). yeong-hwa-ga i-mi si-ja-kaet-ggeo-deun(-yo)

Do you have any tickets left for the 7 o'clock show?

7시 표 아직 있어(요)?

il-gop-ssi pyo a-jik i-sseo(-yo)?

I bought the tickets so you get the popcorn.

예매는 내가 했으니까, 팝콘은 네가 사라.

ye-mae-neun nae-ga hae-sseu-ni-gga, pap-ko-neun ne-ga sa-ra

Two tickets for the 2:30, please.

2시 반 표 두 장 주세요.

du-si ban pyo du jang ju-se-yo

Theater Etiquette

Can I bring some bread into the theater?

영화관에 빵을 좀 가져가도 될까(요)?

yeong-hwa-gwa-ne bbang-eul jom ga-jeo-ga-do
doel-gga(-yo)?

Food is not allowed in the theater.

영화관에서 음식을 먹을 수 없습니다.

yeong-hwa-gwa-ne-seo eum-si-geul meo-geul ssu
eop-sseum-ni-da

Turn your cell phone off before the movie starts.

영화 시작 전에 휴대폰을 꺼 두세요.

yeong-hwa si-jak jeo-ne hyu-dae-po-neul ggeo du-se-yo

Be quiet, please.

조용히 해 주세요.

jo-yong-hi hae ju-se-yo

Please don't kick my seat.

제 자리를 차지 마세요.

je ja-ri-reul cha-ji ma-se-yo

Don't take photos while the movie is showing.

상영 중 촬영 금지.

sang-yeong jung chwa-ryeong geum-ji

Musicals

The performance starts in 20 minutes.

공연은 20분 후에 시작합니다.

gong-yeo-neun i-sip-bbun hu-e si-ja-kam-ni-da

It is a musical for people of all ages.

이 뮤지컬은 모든 관람객이 볼 수 있어(요).

i myu-ji-keo-reun mo-deun gwal-ram-gae-gi bol ssu i-sseo(-yo)

287

What time is the matinee?

마티네는 언제예요?

ma-ti-ne-neun eon-je-ye-yo?

The musical will play for two days on Saturday and Sunday.

그 뮤지컬은 토요일과 일요일 양일간 공연될 예정입니다.

geu myu-ji-keo-reun to-yo-il-gwa i-ryo-il yang-il-gan gong-yeon-doel ye-jeong-im-ni-da

How long is the intermission?

중간 쉬는 시간은 얼마나 돼죠?

jung-gan swi-neun si-ga-neun eol-ma-na dwae-jyo?

Other Theaters

This play is showing three times a day.

이 연극은 하루에 3회 공연해(요).

i yeon-geu-geun ha-ru-e sam-hoe gong-yeon-hae(-yo)

<Romeo and Juliet> is showing at the National Theater.

〈로미오와 줄리엣〉은 지금 국립극장에서 공연 중이에요.

<ro-mi-o-wa jul-ri-e>-seun ji-geum gung-nip-geuk-jjang-e-seo gong-yeon jung-i-e-yo

It's showing regularly at the Civic Center.

시민회관에서 정기 공연이 있어(요).

si-min-hoe-gwa-ne-seo jeong-gi gong-yeo-ni i-sseo(-yo)

Let's go out to dinner and then see <Nanta>.

저녁 식사하고, 〈난타〉 보러 가자.

jeo-nyeok sik-ssa-ha-go, <nan-ta> bo-reo ga-ja

I will be at the concert hall soon.

음악회 홀에 곧 도착할 거예요.

eu-ma-koe ho-re got do-cha-kal ggeo-ye-yo

Bars & Pubs

\# I often get a drink after work.

퇴근 후에 종종 술집에 가(요).

toe-geun hu-e jong-jong sul-jji-be ga(-yo)

\# This bar is my hangout.

이 술집은 내 단골이에요.

i sul-jji-beun nae dan-go-ri-e-yo

\# Shall we prop up the bar?

단골집에 가서 한잔 할까(요)?

dan-gol-jji-be ga-seo han-jan hal-gga(-yo)?

\# This bar is pretty decent!

이 술집 괜찮은데(요)!

i sul-jjip gwaen-cha-neun-de(-yo)!

\# I know a cozy place. Do you want to go?

아늑한 술집 하나 알고 있는데(요). 갈래(요)?

a-neu-kan sul-jjip ha-na al-go in-neun-de(-yo). gal-rae(-yo)?

Do you want to go outside for a smoke?

담배 피우러 나갈래(요)?

dam-bae pi-u-reo na-gal-rae(-yo)?

Let's get a beer!

맥주 한잔 하자!

maek-jju han-jan ha-ja!

I'll buy you a beer when we're done!

일 끝나고 내가 맥주 한잔 쏠게(요)!

il ggeun-na-go nae-ga maek-jju han-jan ssol-gge(-yo)!

That bar has live jazz on the weekends.

이 술집은 주말마다 라이브 재즈 공연이 있어(요).

i sul-jji-beun ju-mal-ma-da ra-i-beu jae-jeu gong-yeo-ni i-sseo(-yo)

What's a good place for live music?

라이브 뮤직이 좋은 곳이 어디예요?

ra-i-beu myu-ji-gi jo-eun go-si eo-di-ye-yo?

Let's go somewhere else!

어디 다른 데로 가자!

eo-di da-reun de-ro ga-ja!

Bar Talk

Cheers!

건배!

geon-bae!

Bottoms up!

원샷!

won-syat!

May I propose a toast?

건배할까(요)?

geon-bae-hal-gga(-yo)?

Here's to your wedding!

두 분의 결혼을 축하하며, 건배!

du bu-ne gyeol-ho-neul chu-ka-ha-myeo, geon-bae!

Can I have another?

한 잔 더 해도 될까(요)?

han jan deo hae-do doel-gga(-yo)?

Do you want one more shot?

한 잔 더 할래(요)?

han jan deo hal-rae(-yo)?

Let's drink some more!

좀 더 마시자!

jom deo ma-si-ja!

Could I pour you a glass?

한 잔 따라 드릴까요?

han jan dda-ra deu-ril-gga-yo?

Let's hit the bottle!

오늘 실컷 마셔(요)!

o-neul sil-keot ma-syeo(-yo)!

Would you like another beer or a shot of whiskey?

맥주 마실래(요) 위스키 마실래(요)?

maek-jju ma sil-rae(-yo) wi-seu-ki ma-sil-rae(-yo)?

Which one do you like, red wine or white wine?

레드와인 좋아해(요) 화이트와인 좋아해(요)?

re-deu-wa-in jo-a-hae(-yo) hwa-i-teu-wa-in jo-a-hae(-yo)?

Two draft beer, please.

생맥주 두 잔 주세요.

saeng-maek-jju du jan ju-se-yo

On second thought, make it a beer.

다시 생각해 보니, 맥주가 좋아(요).

da-si saeng-ga-kae bo-ni, maek-jju-ga jo-a(-yo)

I can't drink hard liquor.

독한 술은 마실 수 없어(요).

do-kan su-reun ma-sil ssu eop-sseo(-yo)

Bar Snacks

What are the cocktails dishes?

무슨 안주가 있어(요)?

mu-seun an-ju-ga i-sseo(-yo)?

Let's order some more side dishes!

안주 더 시켜(요)!

an-ju deo si-kyeo(-yo)!

This goes very well with wine.

이것은 와인과 어울리는 안주예요.

i-geo-seun wa-in-gwa eo-ul-ri-neun an-ju-ye-yo

What would you like to have with your beers?

맥주랑 같이 뭘 드실래요?

maek-jju-rang ga-chi mwol deu-sil-rae-yo?

What's good to eat with 'makkoli?'

'막걸리'와 먹기에 어떤 안주가 좋아(요)?

'mak-ggeol-ri'-wa meok-ggi-e eo-ddeon an-ju-ga jo-a(-yo)?

Stir-fried eel is great with soju.

소주 안주로는 꼼장어 볶음이 최고지(요).

so-ju an-ju-ro-neun ggom-jang-eo bo-ggeu-mi
choe-go-ji(-yo)

The Art Gallery

When is the Daehan Art Gallery open?

대한미술관은 언제 열어(요)?

dae-han-mi-sul-gwa-neun eon-je yeo-reo(-yo)?

The gallery waives its admission fee on Sundays.

그 미술관은 일요일에 무료 입장이에요.

geu mi-sul-gwa-neun i-ryo-i-re mu-ryo ip-jjang-i-e-yo

Is there an entrance fee?

입장료를 받아(요)?

ip-jjang-nyo-reul ba-da(-yo)?

Do you like 'abstract art?' There's an exhibit now at the National Museum.

'추상 미술' 좋아해(요)? 지금 국립미술관에 전시회가 있어(요).

'chu-sang mi-sul' jo-a-hae(-yo)? ji-geum
gung-nip-mi-sul-gwa-ne jeon-si-hoe-ga i-sseo(-yo)

There's nothing to see in this gallery.

이 미술관에는 볼 만한 것이 아무것도
없어(요).

i mi-sul-gwa-ne-neun bol man-han geo-si a-mu-geot-ddo
eop-sseo(-yo)

Museums

One ticket, please

표 한 장 주세요.

pyo han jang ju-se-yo

When does the museum open?

박물관은 언제 열어(요)?

bang-mul-gwa-neun eon-je yeo-reo(-yo)?

There are many thins to see in this museum.

이 박물관에는 다양한 볼거리가 있어(요).

i bang-mul-gwa-ne-neun da-yang-han bol-ggeo-ri-ga
i-sseo(-yo)

Does this museum have an activity program?

이 박물관에는 활동 프로그램이 있어요?

i bang-mul-gwa-ne-neun hwal-ddong peu-ro-geu-rae-mi i-sseo-yo?

This museum has weekend programs for kids.

이 박물관에는 어린이들을 위한 주말 프로그램이 있어(요).

i bang-mul-gwa-ne-neun eo-ri-ni-deu-reul wi-han ju-mal peu-ro-geu-rae-mi i-sseo(-yo)

Do they have audio guides?

오디오 가이드 있어요?

o-di-o ga-i-deu i-sseo-yo?

Admission to the museum is half price after 5 p.m.

오후 5시 이후에는 박물관 입장료가 50% 할인됩니다.

o-hu da-seot-ssi i-hu-e-neun bang-mul-gwan ip-jjang-nyo-ga o-sip-peo-sen-teu ha-rin-doem-ni-da

This museum houses many rare articles.

이 박물관은 희귀 자료를 다수 소장하고
있어(요).

i bang mul-gwa-neun hi-gwi ja-ryo-reul da-su so-jang-ha-go
i-sseo(-yo)

I'm disappointed that the museum is closed.

박물관이 휴관이어서 실망이에요.

bang-mul-gwa-ni hyu-gwa-ni-eo-seo sil-mang-i-e-yo

Does Busan have a science museum?

부산에 과학 박물관 있어(요)?

bu-sa-ne gwa-hak bang-mul-gwan i-sseo(-yo)?

Amusement Parks

Do you like going to amusement parks?

놀이동산에 가는 거 좋아해(요)?

no-ri-dong-sa-ne ga-neun geo jo-a-hae(-yo)?

What kinds of rides do you like?

어떤 놀이기구를 좋아해(요)?

eo-ddeon no-ri-gi-gu-reul jo-a-hae(-yo)?

You're not scared to ride the roller coaster?

롤러코스터 타는 것 안 무서워(요)?

rol-reo-ko-seu-teo ta-neun geot an mu-seo-wo(-yo)?

The merry-go-round is Ye-na's favorite ride.

예나는 회전목마를 가장 좋아해(요).

ye-na-neun hoe-jeon-mong-ma-reul ga-jang jo-a-hae(-yo)

This ticket holder is entitled to enter all areas of the amusement park.

이 표가 있으면, 놀이동산의 모든 것을 이용할 수 있어(요).

i pyo-ga i-sseu-myeon, no-ri-dong-sa-ne mo-deun geo-seul i-yong-hal ssu i-sseo(-yo)

The Fitness Center

How's that gym that you go to?

다니는 헬스클럽은 어때(요)?

da-ni-neun hel-seu-keul-reo-beun eo-ddae(-yo)?

I'll sign up for the gym next month.

다음 달에 헬스클럽에 등록할 거예요.

da-eum da-re hel-seu-keul-reo-be deung-no-kal ggeo-ye-yo

I work out at the gym twice a week.

일주일에 두 번 헬스클럽에서 운동해(요).

il-jju-i-re du beon hel-seu-keul-reo-be-seo un-dong-hae(-yo)

Do they have spinning? Pilates?

자전거 타기 해(요)? 필라테스 해(요)?

ja-jeon-geo ta-gi hae(-yo)? pil-ra-te-seu hae(-yo)?

I need to renew my gym membership.

헬스클럽 회원권을 갱신해야 해(요).

hel-seu-keul-reop hoe-won-ggwo-neul gaeng-sin-hae-ya hae(-yo)

Chapter 4

For My Trip

Booking

Do you have any cheaper tickets?

할인 항공권 있어요?

ha-rin hang-gong-ggwon i-sseo-yo?

What's your destination?

목적지가 어디예요?

mok-jjeok-jji-ga eo-di-ye-yo?

When would you like to leave?

언제 떠날 예정인가요?

eon-je ddeo-nal ye-jeong-in-ga-yo?

One way or round trip?

편도인가요 왕복인가요?

pyeon-do-in-ga-yo wang-bo-gin-ga-yo?

What's the cheapest one way ticket?

가장 싼 편도표는 얼마입니까?

ga-jang ssan pyeon-do-pyo-neun eol-ma-im-ni-gga?

Then give me a round-trip ticket, please.

그럼, 왕복표로 주세요.

geu-reom, wang-bok-pyo-ro ju-se-yo

I'd like to book a flight for Busan.

부산으로 가는 항공권을 예약하려고
하는데요.

bu-sa-neu-ro ga-neun hang-gong-ggwo-neul
ye-ya-ka-ryeo-go ha-neun-de-yo

I want to reserve a seat from Seoul to San Francisco.

서울에서 샌프란시스코로 가는 항공권을
예약하려고요.

seo-u-re-seo saen-peu-ran-si-seu-ko-ro ga-neun
hang-gong-ggwo-neul ye-ya-ka-ryeo-go-yo

Is that the earliest flight you have?

그게 가장 이른 항공편인가요?

geu-ge ga-jang i-reun hang-gong-pyeo-nin-ga-yo?

A one-way ticket to Jeju, please.

제주도행 편도표 한 장 주세요.

je-ju-do-haeng pyeon-do-pyo han jang ju-se-yo

How long is the round trip good for?

왕복표의 유효 기간은 언제까지입니까?

wang-bok-pyo-e yu-hyo gi-ga-neun eon-je-gga-ji-im-ni-gga?

Flight Issues

I'd like to check my reservation.

예약한 항공권을 확인하려고 하는데요.

ye-ya-kan hang-gong-ggwo-neul hwa-gin-ha-ryeo-go
ha-neun-de-yo

How many bags can I check?

가방을 몇 개 가져갈 수 있죠?

ga-bang-eul myeot gae ga-jeo-gal ssu it-jjyo?

I'm on flight 704 to Seoul on December 10.
My reservation number is 123456.

12월 10일 서울로 가는 704편이고,
예약 번호는 123456입니다.

si-bi-wol si-bil seo-ul-ro ga-neun chil-gong-sa-pyeo-ni-go,
ye-yak beon-ho-neun il-i-sam-sa-o-ryu-gim-ni-da

Can I change my flight?

항공편을 바꿀 수 있어요?

hang-gong-pyeo-neul ba-ggul ssu i-sseo-yo?

Can I change my reservation for a later date?

제 예약 날짜를 미룰 수 있어요?

je ye-yak nal-jja-reul mi-rul ssu i-sseo-yo?

Passports

I'd like to apply for a passport.

여권을 만들려고요.

yeo-ggwo-neul man-deul-ryeo-go-yo

Where can I get a passport?

여권을 발급하려면 어디로 가야 하나요?

yeo-ggwo-neul bal-geu-pa-ryeo-myeon eo-di-ro ga-ya
ha-na-yo?

What should I prepare to get a passport?

여권을 발급하려면 무엇을 준비해야 하나요?

yeo-ggwo-neul bal-geu-pa-ryeo-myeon mu-eo-seul
jun-bi-hae-ya ha-na-yo?

How long does it take to get a passport?

여권을 만드는 데 얼마나 걸려요?

yeo-ggwo-neul man-deu-neun de eol-ma-na geol-ryeo-yo?

My passport expires at the end of the year.

제 여권은 올해 말로 만기가 됩니다.

je yeo-ggwo-neun ol-hae mal-ro man-gi-ga doem-ni-da

Visas

I want to apply for a visa for the Republic of Korea.

한국 비자를 신청하려고 하는데요.

han-guk bi-ja-reul sin-cheong-ha-ryeo-go ha-neun-de-yo

You don't need a visa to travel to Jeju.

제주도를 관광할 때 비자가 필요 없습니다.

je-ju-do-reul gwan-gwang-hal ddae bi-ja-ga pi-ryo
eop-sseum-ni-da

How long does it take to get a visa?

비자를 신청하는 데 얼마나 걸립니까?

bi-ja-reul sin-cheong-ha-neun de eol-ma-na geol-rim-ni-gga?

This visa is good for 30 days only.

이 비자의 유효 기간은 30일입니다.

i bi-ja-e yu-hyo gi-ga-neun sam-si-bi-rim-ni-da

I want to know if my visa has been authorized yet.

비자가 발급되었는지 물어보려고요.

bi-ja-ga bal-geup-ddoe-eon-neun-ji mu-reo-bo-ryeo-go-yo

I'm planning to go to Hong Kong for travel. Do I need a visa?

홍콩으로 여행 가려는데요.
비자가 필요합니까?

hong-kong-eu-ro yeo-haeng ga-ryeo-neun-de-yo.
bi-ja-ga pi-ryo-ham-ni-gga?

Without a visa, you can stay in Hong Kong for 90 days.

홍콩은 90일 간 비자 면제입니다.

hong-kong-eun gu-si-bil gan bi-ja myeon-je-im-ni-da

Please renew your visa before it expires.

비자 만료 기간 전에 갱신해야 합니다.

bi-ja mal-ryo gi-gan jeo-ne gaeng-sin-hae-ya ham-ni-da

What is your visa status?

비자가 어떤 종류입니까?

bi-ja-ga eo-ddeon jong-nyu-im-ni-gga?

I see you have a student visa.

알고 보니 학생 비자였군요.

al-go bo-ni hak-ssaeng bi-ja-yeot-ggun-yo

The Airport

Please check in at least 2 hours before your departure time.

늦어도 이륙하기 두 시간 전에 탑승 수속해야 합니다.

neu-jeo-do i-ryu-ka-gi du si-gan jeo-ne tap-sseung su-so-kae-ya ham-ni-da

What time did you arrive at the airport?

공항에는 몇 시에 도착했어(요)?

gong-hang-e-neun myeot si-e do-cha-kae-sseo(-yo)?

Where is the international terminal?

국제선 터미널은 어디입니까?

guk-jje-seon teo-mi-neo-reun eo-di-im-ni-gga?

\# I missed my connection because my flight was delayed.

비행기가 연착되는 바람에, 연결편을 놓쳤어(요).

bi-haeng-gi-ga yeon-chak-ddoe-neun ba-ra-me, yeon-gyeol-pyeo-neul not-cheo-sseo(-yo)

\# I reached the airport in the nick of time.

공항에 아슬아슬하게 도착했어(요).

gong-hang-e a-seu-ra-seul-ha-ge do-cha-kae-sseo(-yo)

Check-in

\# Where is the Asiana Airlines office?

아시아나항공 카운터는 어디예요?

a-si-a-na-hang-gong ka-un-teo-neun eo-di-ye-yo?

\# You may proceed to the next window.

다음 창구로 가세요.

da-eum chang-gu-ro ga-se-yo

I reserved a flight ticket on the Internet.

인터넷에서 항공권을 예약했습니다.

in-teo-ne-se-seo hang-gong-ggwo-neul
ye-ya-kaet-sseum-ni-da

I will probably pay for the extra-baggage charge.

초과 수하물 요금을 내야 할 거예요.

cho-gwa su-ha-mul yo-geu-meul nae-ya hal ggeo-ye-yo

When is the check-in?

체크인 시간이 언제예요?

che-keu-in si-ga-ni eon-je-ye-yo?

Departure Check

May I see your passport, please?

여권을 보여 주시겠어요?

yeo-ggwo-neul bo-yeo ju-si-ge-sseo-yo?

Where are you headed?

어디에 가십니까?

eo-di-e ga-sim-ni-gga?

I'm on my way to Yeo-su.

여수에 갑니다.

yeo-su-e gam-ni-da

When are you going to return?

언제 귀국합니까?

eon-je gwi-gu-kam-ni-gga?

Who is going with you?

일행이 있습니까?

il-haeng-i it-sseum-ni-gga?

I'm going with my boss.

상사와 함께 갑니다.

sang-sa-wa ham-gge gam-ni-da

Duty-free

Where are the duty-free shops?

면세점은 어디 있어(요)?

myeon-se-jeo-meun eo-di i-sseo(-yo)?

Duty-free shops are on the departures level.

면세점은 출발층에 있어(요).

myeon-se-jeo-meun chul-bal-cheung-e i-sseo(-yo)

Will we have time to do some duty-free shopping?

면세점 쇼핑할 시간 있어(요)?

myeon-se-jeom syo-ping-hal si-gan i-sseo(-yo)?

I think you're over the limit.

한도 초과한 거 같은데(요).

han-do cho-gwa-han geo ga-teun-de(-yo)

How much alcohol am I allowed to buy?

주류는 얼마나 살 수 있어(요)?

ju-ryu-neun eol-ma-na sal ssu i-sseo(-yo)?

I have to buy some gifts for my family at a duty-free shop in the airport.

공항 면세점에서 가족 선물을 사야 해(요).

gong-hang myeon-se-jeo-me-seo ga-jok seon-mu-reul sa-ya hae(-yo)

Boarding

When should I check in?

언제 탑승합니까?

eon-je tap-sseung-ham-ni-gga?

Which gate do I go to?

어느 탑승구로 가야 합니까?

eo-neu tap-sseung-gu-ro ga-ya ham-ni-gga?

We will begin boarding soon.

곧 탑승을 시작하겠습니다.

got tap-sseung-eul si-ja-ka-get-sseum-ni-da

May I see your boarding pass, please?

탑승권을 보여 주시겠어요?

tap-sseung-ggwo-neul bo-yeo ju-si-ge-sseo-yo?

Flight 605, departing at 10 a.m., has had a gate change. The new gate is B29.

오전 10시에 출발하는 605편의 탑승구가 B29로 변경되었습니다.

o-jeon yeol-ssi-e chul-bal-ha-neun yuk-ggong-o-pyeo-ne tap-sseung-gu-ga bi-i-sip-ggu-ro byeon-gyeong-doe-eot-sseum-ni-da

Immigration

This is my first visit.

이번이 처음 방문입니다.

i-beo-ni cheo-eum bang-mu-nim-ni-da

I'm here to visit my relatives.

친척들을 만나러 왔습니다.

chin-cheok-ddeu-reul man-na-reo wat-sseum-ni-da

I'll stay for a week.

일주일 머물 겁니다.

il-jju-il meo-mul ggeom-ni-da

I'll be staying at the Seoul Hotel.

서울 호텔에 묵을 겁니다.

seo-ul ho-te-re mu-geul ggeom-ni-da

I'm just here for sightseeing.

관광차 왔습니다.

gwan-gwang-cha wat-sseum-ni-da

I'm here on business.

사업차 왔습니다.

sa-eop-cha wat-sseum-ni-da

I'm traveling with my friend.

친구와 여행 왔습니다.

chin-gu-wa yeo-haeng wat-sseum-ni-da

Baggage

Where can I pick up my baggage?

어디에서 짐을 찾습니까?

eo-di-e-seo ji-meul chat-sseum-ni-gga?

My baggage has got damaged.

제 짐이 파손됐어요.

je ji-mi pa-son-dwae-sseo-yo

I can't find my baggage.

제 짐을 못 찾겠어요.

je ji-meul mot chat-gge-sseo-yo

Can you check to see where my baggage is?

제 짐이 어디에 있는지 확인해 주세요.

je ji-mi eo-di-e in-neun-ji hwa-gin-hae ju-se-yo

My baggage hasn't arrived yet.

제 짐이 아직 도착하지 않았어요.

je ji-mi a-jik do-cha-ka-ji a-na-sseo-yo

Can you deliver it to my hotel?

호텔까지 운반해 주실 수 있어요?

ho-tel-gga-ji un-ban-hae ju-sil ssu i-sseo-yo?

Customs

Please fill in this customs declaration.

세관 신고서를 기입해 주세요.

se-gwan sin-go-seo-reul gi-i-pae ju-se-yo

Can I see your customs declaration?

세관 신고서를 보여 주시겠어요?

se-gwan sin-go-seo-reul bo-yeo ju-si-ge-sseo-yo?

Anything to declare?

신고할 물품이 있습니까?

sin-go-hal mul-pu-mi it-sseum-ni-gga?

Nothing to declare.

신고할 것이 없습니다.

sin-go-hal ggeo-si eop-sseum-ni-da

It's for my own use.

이것은 제가 쓰는 것입니다.

i-geo-seun je-ga sseu-neun geo-sim-ni-da

Can I bring this?

이것을 반입할 수 있어요?

i-geo-seul ba-ni-pal ssu i-sseo-yo?

Meeting at the Airport

Will someone pick you up at the airport?

누가 공항에 마중 나와(요)?

nu-ga gong-hang-e ma-jung na-wa(-yo)?

Can you meet me at the airport?

공항에 마중 나올 수 있어(요)?

gong-hang-e ma-jung na-ol ssu i-sseo(-yo)?

I'll arrange for a car to meet you at the airport.

당신을 마중하려고 차를 예약했어요.

dang-si-neul ma-jung-ha-ryeo-go cha-reul ye-ya-kae-sseo-yo

Thanks for meeting me.

마중하러 공항에 와서 고마워(요).

ma-jung-ha-reo gong-hang-e wa-seo go-ma-wo(-yo)

I'll be there. When do you land?

마중 나갈게(요). 언제 내려(요)?

ma-jung na-gal-gge(-yo). eon-je nae-ryeo(-yo)?

I need to pick up my sister at the airport.

공항에 여동생을 마중 나가야 해(요).

gong-hang-e yeo-dong-saeng-eul ma-jung na-ga-ya hae(-yo)

On Board

\# Could you help me find my seat?

좌석을 안내해 주시겠어요?

jwa-seo-geul an-nae-hae ju-si-ge-sseo-yo?

\# This way, please. Your seat is just over there.

이쪽으로 오세요. 바로 저기입니다.

i-jjo-geu-ro o-se-yo. ba-ro jeo-gi-im-ni-da

\# Can you help me with my bag?

제 가방 좀 도와주실래요?

je ga-bang jom do-wa-ju-sil-rae-yo?

\# I don't think it'll fit in the overhead bin.

그건 기내 짐칸에 들어갈 것 같지 않은데요.

geu-geon gi-nae jim-ka-ne deu-reo-gal ggeot gat-jji
a-neun-de-yo

Please fasten your seat belt.

안전벨트를 매 주십시오.

an-jeon-bel-teu-reul mae ju-sip-ssi-o

Do they sell duty-free goods on board?

기내에서 면세품을 판매하나요?

gi-nae-e-seo myeon-se-pu-meul pan-mae-ha-na-yo?

May I have a pillow and a blanket?

베개와 담요를 주실래요?

be-gae-wa dam-nyo-reul ju-sil-rae-yo?

How long does the flight take?

비행시간은 얼마나 돼요?

bi-haeng-si-ga-neun eol-ma-na dwae-yo?

What's the time difference between Seoul and New York?

서울과 뉴욕의 시차는 얼마나 돼(요)?

seo-ul-gwa nyu-yo-ge si-cha-neun eol-ma-na dwae(-yo)?

The toilet is vacant now.

화장실이 지금 비었어(요).

hwa-jang-si-ri ji-geum bi-eo-sseo(-yo)

Excuse me, would you mind trading seats with me?

죄송하지만, 저와 자리를 바꿔 주실 수 있어요?

joe-song-ha-ji-man, jeo-wa ja-ri-reul ba-ggwo ju-sil ssu i-sseo-yo?

I don't like the in-flight movies.

기내 영화가 마음에 안 들어(요).

gi-nae yeong-hwa-ga ma-eu-me an deu-reo(-yo)

In-flight Meals

Is there a meal on this flight?

기내식이 나오나요?

gi-nae-si-gi na-o-na-yo?

Can I get something to drink?

음료수를 좀 주시겠어요?

eum-nyo-su-reul jom ju-si-ge-sseo-yo?

Which would you prefer, beef or fish?

소고기와 생선 중, 어떤 것으로
하시겠습니까?

so-go-gi-wa saeng-seon jung, eo-ddeon geo-seu-ro
ha-si-get-sseum-ni-gga?

Beef, please.

소고기로 할게요.

so-go-gi-ro hal-gge-yo

How was your meal?

기내식 괜찮았어(요)?

gi-nae-sik gwaen-cha-na-sseo(-yo)?

I'd like to have a glass of water, please.

물 한 잔 주세요.

mul han jan ju-se-yo

Booking a Room

\# I'd like to book a room.

방을 예약하려고 하는데요.

bang-eul ye-ya-ka-ryeo-go ha-neun-de-yo

\# Sorry, but we're full.

죄송합니다만, 만실입니다.

joe-song-ham-ni-da-man, man-si-rim-ni-da

\# I'd like to make a reservation for 2 nights
next week.

다음 주에 2박을 예약하고 싶어요.

da-eum ju-e i-ba-geul ye-ya-ka-go si-peo-yo

\# I'd like a double room with a bath.

욕실이 딸린 더블룸으로 하려고요.

yok-ssi-ri ddal-rin deo-beul-ru-meu-ro ha-ryeo-go-yo

Do you have a single room available?

싱글룸 있어요?

sing-geul-rum i-sseo-yo?

I'd rather stay closer to downtown.

차라리 시내에 있는 호텔에 머물겠어(요).

cha-ra-ri si-nae-e in-neun ho-te-re meo-mul-ge-sseo(-yo)

I'd like a room with a view of the ocean.

바다가 보이는 방으로 부탁합니다.

ba-da-ga bo-i-neun bang-eu-ro bu-ta-kam-ni-da

I'd like to stay 3 nights and check out Sunday morning.

3박하고 일요일 오전에 체크아웃하려고요.

sam-ba-ka-go i-ryo-il o-jeo-ne che-keu-a-u-ta-ryeo-go-yo

What's the rate for the room?

숙박비가 얼마예요?

suk-bbak-bbi-ga eol-ma-ye-yo?

Does this rate include breakfast?

조식이 포함됐어요?

jo-si-gi po-ham-dwae-sseo-yo?

Do you have a room cheaper?

좀 더 싼 방 있어(요)?

jom deo ssan bang i-sseo(-yo)?

It had some good reviews online.

인터넷에 좋은 후기가 좀 있었어(요).

in-teo-ne-se jo-eun hu-gi-ga jom i-sseo-sseo(-yo)

Checking In

Can I check in now?

지금 체크인할 수 있어요?

ji-geum che-keu-in-hal ssu i-sseo-yo?

What time is check-in?

몇 시에 체크인할 수 있어요?

myeot si-e che-keu-in-hal ssu i-sseo-yo?

When is the earliest I can check in?

가장 빨리 체크인할 수 있는 게 언제예요?

ga-jang bbal-ri che-keu-in-hal ssu in-neun ge eon-je-ye-yo?

Do you have a reservation?

예약하셨습니까?

ye-ya-ka-syeot-sseum-ni-gga?

My name is Min-ji Go. I have a reservation for a single room.

싱글룸 예약한 고민지입니다.

sing-geul-rum ye-ya-kan go-min-ji-im-ni-da

I booked online.

인터넷에서 예약했습니다.

in-teo-ne-se-seo ye-ya-kaet-sseum-ni-da

I need to change my check-in date.

체크인 날짜를 변경해야 해(요).

che-keu-in nal-jja-reul byeon-gyeong-hae-ya hae(-yo)

I'll call the hotel and cancel.

호텔에 전화해서 취소하겠다고 할게(요).

ho-te-re jeon-hwa-hae-seo chwi-so-ha-get-dda-go

hal-gge(-yo)

Can I check in early?

조기 체크인이 가능해(요)?

jo-gi che-keu-i-ni ga-neung-hae(-yo)?

Do you need a credit card for a damage deposit when I check in?

체크인할 때 디포짓을 위한 신용카드가

필요해요?

che-keu-in-hal ddae di-po-ji-seul wi-han si-nyong-ka-deu-ga

pi-ryo-hae-yo?

Could you help me with my bags?

짐을 맡길 수 있어요?

ji-meul mat-ggil ssu i-sseo-yo?

Checking Out

We'd like to check out.

체크아웃하려고요.

che-keu-a-u-ta-ryeo-go-yo

I'll probably check out around 10.

10시쯤 체크아웃하려고요.

yeol-ssi-jjeum che-keu-a-u-ta-ryeo-go-yo

Is it possible to have a late check out?

늦은 체크아웃 가능해(요)?

neu-jeun che-keu-a-ut ga-neung-hae(-yo)?

I already paid the hotel bill.

청구서를 지불했어요.

cheong-gu-seo-reul ji-bul-hae-sseo-yo

What's this item?

이 항목은 뭐죠?

i hang-mo-geun mwo-jyo?

I never ordered any room service.

룸서비스를 시키지 않았는데요.

rum-seo-bi-seu-reul si-ki-ji a-nan-neun-de-yo

I think there is a mistake here.

여기가 잘못된 것 같은데요.

yeo-gi-ga jal-mot-ddoen geot ga-teun-de-yo

Hotel Services

Do you have a laundry service?

세탁 서비스가 되나요?

se-tak seo-bi-seu-ga doe-na-yo?

When will the sauna open?

사우나는 언제 열어요?

sa-u-na-neun eon-je yeo-reo-yo?

Does the room have a security box?

방에 금고가 있어요?

bang-e geum-go-ga i-sseo-yo?

I'd like a wake-up call at 6, please.

아침 6시에 모닝콜을 해 주세요.

a-chim yeo-seot-ssi-e mo-ning-ko-reul hae ju-se-yo

Can you hold my bags until my flight time?

이 짐을 비행기 시간까지 맡아 줄 수
있어요?

i ji-meul bi-haeng-gi si-gan-gga-ji ma-ta jul ssu i-sseo-yo?

Can I have my key?

제 방 열쇠를 주시겠어요?

je bang yeol-soe-reul ju-si-ge-sseo-yo?

Is there any message for me?

제게 메시지 온 것 있어요?

je-ge me-si-ji on geot i-sseo-yo?

I'd like to stay one day longer.

하루 연장하려고 하는데요.

ha-ru yeon-jang-ha-ryeo-go ha-neun-de-yo

Could someone change my towels?

수건을 바꿔 줄 수 있어요?

su-geo-neul ba-ggwo jul ssu i-sseo-yo?

What amenities do you have in this hotel?

이 호텔에 어떤 편의 시설이 있어요?

i ho-te-re eo-ddeon pyeo-ni si-seo-ri i-sseo-yo?

I'm having trouble with my key card.

카드키에 문제가 있어요.

ka-deu-ki-e mun-je-ga i-sseo-yo

What's the Wi-Fi password?

와이파이 비밀번호가 뭐예요?

wa-i-pa-i bi-mil-beon-ho-ga mwo-ye-yo?

Troubles at the Hotel

I left the key in my room.

열쇠를 방에 두고 나왔어요.

yeol-soe-reul bang-e du-go na-wa-sseo-yo

My room is too close to the elevator.
Can I change it?

방이 엘리베이터와 너무 가까워서요.
바꿀 수 있을까요?

bang-i el-ri-be-i-teo-wa neo-mu ga-gga-wo-seo-yo.
ba-ggul ssu i-sseul-gga-yo?

There's no hot water.

방에 온수가 나오지 않아요.

bang-e on-su-ga na-o-ji a-na-yo

The toilet doesn't flush.

변기가 막혔어요.

byeon-gi-ga ma-kyeo-sseo-yo

My room has not been cleaned yet.

방이 청소되어 있지 않아요.

bang-i cheong-so-doe-eo it-jji a-na-yo

It's very noisy next door.

옆 방이 시끄러워 죽겠어요.

yeop bang-i si-ggeu-reo-wo juk-gge-sseo-yo

Tourist Information

\# Where is the tourist information center?

관광안내소가 어디에 있습니까?

gwan-gwang-an-nae-so-ga eo-di-e it-sseum-ni-gga?

\# Do you have any leaflets on the town?

시내 관광 안내서 있어요?

si-nae gwan-gwang an-nae-seo i-sseo-yo?

\# Can you recommend some interesting places around here?

근처에 가 볼 만한 관광지를 추천해 주실래요?

geun-cheo-e ga bol man-han gwan-gwang-ji-reul chu-cheon-hae ju-sil-rae-yo?

\# Please recommend a cheap and nice hotel.

싸고 좋은 호텔을 추천해 주세요.

ssa-go jo-eun ho-te-reul chu-cheon-hae ju-se-yo

340

Could you draw me a map?

약도를 그려 주실 수 있어요?

yak-ddo-reul geu-ryeo ju-sil ssu i-sseo-yo?

Tour Inquiries

What time does the next tour leave?

다음 투어는 언제 출발해요?

da-eum tu-eo-neun eon-je chul-bal-hae-yo?

Do you have any one-day tours?

당일치기 여행 있어요?

dang-il-chi-gi yeo-haeng i-sseo-yo?

What time and where does it leave?

몇 시, 어디에서 출발해요?

myeot si, eo-di-e-seo chul-bal-hae-yo?

How long does it take?

몇 시간 걸려요?

myeot si-gan geol-ryeo-yo?

What time will we be back?
몇 시에 돌아올 수 있어요?
myeot si-e do-ra-ol ssu i-sseo-yo?

How much is it per person?
1인당 비용이 얼마예요?
i-rin-dang bi-yong-i eol-ma-ye-yo?

Do you have a guide?
관광 가이드가 있어요?
gwan-gwang ga-i-deu-ga i-sseo-yo?

I'd like to book a city tour.
시내 관광을 예약하고 싶은데요.
si-nae gwan-gwang-eul ye-ya-ka-go si-peun-de-yo

Do you have any tours to Gyeongbokgung Palace?
경복궁 관광 투어가 있어요?
gyeong-bok-ggung gwan-gwang tu-eo-ga i-sseo-yo?

Do you have a tour for night views?

야경을 볼 수 있어요?

ya-gyeong-eul bol ssu i-sseo-yo?

Is lunch included?

점심이 포함되어 있나요?

jeom-si-mi po-ham-doe-eo in-na-yo?

Is there one leaving in the morning?

아침에 출발하는 것이 있어요?

a-chi-me chul-bal-ha-neun geo-si i-sseo-yo?

Purchasing Tickets

Where can I buy a ticket?

어디에서 입장권을 사요?

eo-di-e-seo ip-jjang-ggwo-neul sa-yo?

How much is the admission fee?

입장권이 얼마예요?

ip-jjang-ggwo-ni eol-ma-ye-yo?

Two adults and one child, please.

어른 두 장, 어린이 한 장 주세요.

eo-reun du jang, eo-ri-ni han jang ju-se-yo

Do you have any tickets for the 1 o'clock performance?

1시 공연, 자리 있습니까?

han si gong-yeon, ja-ri it-sseum-ni-gga?

Are there any tickets left for tonight's show?

오늘 밤 공연 입장권 남은 게 있어요?

o-neul bam gong-yeon ip-jjang-ggwon na-meun ge
i-sseo-yo?

Do you have a group discount?

단체 할인돼요?

dan-che ha-rin-dwae-yo?

344

Watching & Enjoying

What a beautiful place!

정말 아름다운 곳이네요!

jeong-mal a-reum-da-un go-si-ne-yo!

What a fantastic view!

전망이 환상적이에요!

jeon-mang-i hwan-sang-jeo-gi-e-yo!

What time will it be over?

관람 시간은 몇 시에 끝나요?

gwal-ram si-ga-neun myeot si-e ggeun-na-yo?

It's not recommended for children.

어린이는 이용할 수 없습니다.

eo-ri-ni-neun i-yong-hal ssu eop-sseum-ni-da

Can I take a look inside?

내부를 둘러봐도 되나요?

nae-bu-ruel dul-reo-bwa-do doe-na-yo?

Where is the souvenir shop?

기념품 가게는 어디 있습니까?

gi-nyeom-pum ga-ge-neun eo-di it-sseum-ni-gga?

Where is the exit?

출구가 어디 있습니까?

chul-gu-ga eo-di it-sseum-ni-gga?

Asking the Way

Which way do I go to get to the National Gallery?

국립미술관은 어떻게 갑니까?

gung-nip-mi-sul-gwa-neun eo-ddeo-ke gam-ni-gga?

Is this the right way to N Seoul Tower?

N 서울 타워에 가려면 이 길이 맞아요?

en seo-ul ta-wo-e ga-ryeo-myeon i gi-ri ma-ja-yo?

Please tell me the way to the bus stop.

버스 정류소로 가는 길을 알려 주세요.

beo-seu jeong-nyu-so-ro ga-neun gi-reul al-ryeo ju-se-yo

Is there a subway station around here?

근처에 지하철역이 있습니까?

geun-cheo-e ji-ha-cheol-ryeo-gi it-sseum-ni-gga?

It's far from here. You'd better take a bus.

여기에서 멀어요. 버스를 타고 가는 편이
좋겠어요.

yeo-gi-e-seo meo-reo-yo. beo-seu-reul ta-go ga-neun
pyeo-ni jo-ke-sseo-yo

How far is the museum from here?

여기에서 박물관까지 멀어요?

yeo-gi-e-seo bang-mul-gwan-gga-ji meo-reo-yo?

Is it far from hotel?

호텔에서 멀어요?

ho-te-re-seo meo-reo-yo?

Can I walk there?

걸어서 갈 수 있어요?

geo-reo-seo gal ssu i-sseo-yo?

How long does it take by foot?

걸어서 가면 몇 분 걸립니까?

geo-reo-seo ga-myeon myeot bun geol-rim-ni-gga?

It's only 5 minutes' walk.

걸어서 5분이면 도착합니다.

geo-reo-seo o-bu-ni-myeon do-cha-kam-ni-da

I'm sorry, I'm a stranger here.

죄송하지만, 저도 여기는 처음입니다.

joe-song-ha-ji-man, jeo-do yeo-gi-neun cheo-eu-mim-ni-da

Trains

\# One round trip to Jeonju, please.

전주로 가는 왕복표 한 장 주세요.

jeon-ju-ro ga-neun wang-bok-pyo han jang ju-se-yo

\# The train was 30 minutes behind schedule.

기차가 30분 연착됐어요.

gi-cha-ga sam-sip-bbun yeon-chak-ddwae-sseo-yo

\# What time is the first train to Yongsan?

용산행 첫 차가 몇 시에 있죠?

yong-san-haeng cheot cha-ga myeot si-e it-jjyo?

\# How often does the train come?

배차 간격이 어떻게 돼죠?

bae-cha gan-gyeo-gi eo-ddeo-ke dwae-jyo?

\# Every 30 minutes.

30분마다 있습니다.

sam-sip-bbun-ma-da it-sseum-ni-da

What time does the train for Gwangju leave?

광주행 기차가 몇 시에 출발하죠?

gwang-ju-haeng gi-cha-ga myeot si-e chul-bal-ha-jyo?

Subways

Where is the ticket counter?

매표소가 어디예요?

mae-pyo-so-ga eo-di-ye-yo?

Can I have a subway map?

지하철 노선도 한 장 주실래요?

ji-ha-cheol no-seon-do han jang ju-sil-rae-yo?

Where should I transfer?

어디에서 갈아타나요?

eo-di-e-seo ga-ra-ta-na-yo?

You should transfer to line 2.

2호선으로 갈아타세요.

i-ho-seo-neu-ro ga-ra-ta-se-yo

How much is the fare?

요금은 얼마예요?

yo-geu-meun eol-ma-ye-yo?

Which exit should I take for Yeouido Park?

여의도공원으로 가려면 몇 번 출구로 가야
해요?

yeo-i-do-gong-wo-neu-ro ga-ryeo-myeon myeot beon
chul-gu-ro ga-ya hae-yo?

Buses

Where is the nearest bus stop?

가장 가까운 버스 정류장이 어디예요?

ga-jang ga-gga-un beo-seu jeong-nyu-jang-i eo-di-ye-yo?

Does this bus go to the airport?

이 버스는 공항에 갑니까?

i beo-seu-neun gong-hang-e gam-ni-gga?

Could you tell me where to get off?

어디에서 내려야 하는지 알려 줄 수 있어요?

eo-di-e-seo nae-ryeo-ya ha-neun-ji al-ryeo jul ssu i-sseo-yo?

Is this seat vacant?

여기에 자리 있어요?

yeo-gi-e ja-ri i-sseo-yo?

I'll get off here.

여기에서 내리겠습니다.

yeo-gi-e-seo nae-ri-get-sseum-ni-da

Press this button when you want to get off.

버스에서 내릴 때, 이 버튼을 누르세요.

beo-seu-e-seo nae-ril ddae, i beo-teu-neul nu-reu-se-yo

I missed the last bus.

막차를 놓쳤어요.

mak-cha-reul not-cheo-sseo-yo

Do you sell tickets for the airport shuttle bus?

공항 셔틀버스 표 팔아요?

gong-hang syeo-teul-beo-seu pyo pa-ra-yo?

How often does the airport bus operate?

공항버스는 얼마나 자주 운행돼죠?

gong-hang-beo-seu-neun eol-ma-na ja-ju
un-haeng-dwae-jyo?

When's the last bus to Bundang?

분당으로 가는 막차는 몇 시에 있나요?

bun-dang-eu-ro ga-neun mak-cha-neun myeot si-e in-na-yo?

Do you ride this bus often?

이 버스 자주 타세요?

i beo-seu ja-ju ta-se-yo?

I'll go to Daejeon by express bus.

고속버스를 타고 대전에 갈 거예요.

go-sok-bbeo-seu-reul ta-go dae-jeo-ne gal ggeo-ye-yo

Taxis

Could you call me a taxi, please?

택시를 불러 주실래요?

taek-ssi-reul bul-reo ju-sil-rae-yo?

Let's catch a taxi here!

여기에서 택시를 잡자!

yeo-gi-e-seo taek-ssi-reul jap-jja!

I can't find a taxi.

택시를 못 잡겠어요.

taek-ssi-reul mot jap-gge-sseo-yo

Take me to this address, please.

이 주소로 가 주세요.

i ju-so-ro ga ju-se-yo

Airport, please.

공항으로 가 주세요.

gong-hang-eu-ro ga ju-se-yo

Step on it, please.

빨리 가 주세요.

bbal-ri ga ju-se-yo

Slow down, please.

천천히 가 주세요.

cheon-cheon-hi ga ju-se-yo

I called a taxi 30 minutes ago, but it hasn't arrived.

택시를 부른 지 30분이 지났는데, 아직 안 왔어(요).

taek-ssi-reul bu-reun ji sam-sip-bbu-ni ji-nat-neun-de, a-jik an wa-sseo(-yo)

Drop me off at the corner.

저 모퉁이에서 내릴게요.

jeo mo-tung-i-e-seo nae-ril-gge-yo

Can you take out my bags?

제 짐을 꺼내 주실래요?

je ji-meul ggeo-nae ju-sil-rae-yo?

I had a heck of a time flagging down a taxi.

택시 잡느라고 혼났어(요).

taek-ssi jap-neu-ra-go hon-na-sseo(-yo)

Please get a taxi on the other side of the street.

길 건너편에서 택시를 타세요.

gil geon-neo-pyeo-ne-seo taek-ssi-reul ta-se-yo

Keep the change.

잔돈은 가지세요.

jan-do-neun ga-ji-se-yo

Ships & Cruises

Where can I take a sightseeing boat?

유람선 타는 데가 어디예요?

yu-ram-seon ta-neun de-ga eo-di-ye-yo?

\# Let's go on a cruise down the Han River after lunch!

점심 먹고 한강 유람선을 타자!

jeom-sim meok-ggo han-gang yu-ram-seo-neul ta-ja!

\# I get seasick whenever I get in a boat.

배를 탈 때마다 뱃멀미를 해(요).

bae-reul tal ddae-ma-da baen-meol-mi-reul hae(-yo)

\# What time do we embark?

승선 시간은 몇 시입니까?

seung-seon si-ga-neun myeot si-im-ni-gga?

\# We just got back from a cruise.

유람선 여행에서 막 돌아왔어(요).

yu-ram-seon yeo-haeng-e-seo mak do-ra-wa-sseo(-yo)

\# How about going on a cruise?

유람선 여행은 어때(요)?

yu-ram-seon yeo-haeng-eun eo-ddae(-yo)?

Chapter 5

Tough Times

Emergency

\# This is an emergency.

응급 상황이에요.

eung-geup sang-hwang-i-e-yo

\# My friend fell and is unconscious.

친구가 쓰러져서 의식이 없어(요).

chin-gu-ga sseu-reo-jeo-seo ui-si-gi eop-sseo(-yo)

\# I think he's having a heart attack.

그는 심장마비인 거 같아(요).

geu-neun sim-jang-ma-bi-in geo ga-ta(-yo)

\# We have to give first aid to him right now.

당장 그에게 응급 처치를 해야 해(요).

dang-jang geu-e-ge eung-geup cheo-chi-reul hae-ya hae(-yo)

\# Do you have a cell phone? Quick, call 119!

휴대폰 있어(요)? 얼른, 119에 전화해(요)!

hyu-dae-pon i-sseo(-yo)? eol-reun, il-ril-gu-e
jeon-hwa-hae(-yo)!

360

Ambulance

Could you call an ambulance?

구급차를 불러 주실래요?

gu-geup-cha-reul bul-reo ju-sil-rae-yo?

Hurry and call an ambulance.

어서 구급차를 불러라.

eo-seo gu-geup-cha-reul bul-reo-ra

Don't move until the ambulance arrives.

구급차가 오기 전에 움직이지 마(세요).

gu-geup-cha-ga o-gi jeo-ne um-ji-gi-ji ma(-se-yo)

Here comes an ambulance.

구급차가 와(요).

gu-geup-cha-ga wa(-yo)

Is there anything I can do before the ambulance comes?

구급차가 오기 전에 제가 뭘 할 수 있을까요?

gu-geup-cha-ga o-gi jeo-ne je-ga mwol hal ssu i-sseul-gga-yo?

Luckily an ambulance arrived shortly after.

다행히 구급차가 금방 왔어(요).

da-haeng-i gu-geup-cha-ga geum-bang wa-sseo(-yo)

Emergency Room

Where's the emergency room, please?

응급실이 어디예요?

eung-geup-ssi-ri eo-di-ye-yo?

Go to your local hospital emergency room.

집에서 가까운 병원 응급실로 가세요.

ji-be-seo ga-gga-un byeong-won eung-geup-ssil-ro ga-se-yo

Should I go to the E.R. now or just schedule a doctor's appointment tomorrow morning?

지금 응급실로 가야 할까(요) 아니면 내일 아침 병원 진료를 예약할까(요)?

ji-geum eung-geup-ssil-ro ga-ya hal-gga(-yo) a-ni-myeon nae-il a-chim byeong-won jil-ryo-reul ye-ya-kal-gga(-yo)?

My son was rushed to the emergency room. He had an allergic reaction.

우리 아들은 급하게 응급실에 갔어(요).
알레르기 반응이 있었거든(요).

u-ri a-deu-reun geu-pa-ge eung-geup-ssi-re ga-sseo(-yo).
al-re-reu-gi ban-eung-i i-sseot-ggeo-deun(-yo)

Getting Lost

I got lost.

길을 잃었어(요).

gi-reul i-reo-sseo(-yo)

Where are you now?

지금 어디에 있어(요)?

ji-geum eo-di-e i-sseo(-yo)?

We're going the wrong way.

길을 잘못 들어선 거 같아(요).

gi-reul jal-mot deu-reo-seon geo ga-ta(-yo)

I don't know where I am.

어디에 있는지 모르겠어(요).

eo-di-e in-neun-ji mo-reu-ge-sseo(-yo)

Can you tell me what you can see around you?

주변에 뭐가 있는지 말씀해 주시겠어요?

ju-byeo-ne mwo-ga in-neun-ji mal-sseum-hae
ju-si-ge-sseo-yo?

Where can I find this address?

여기 주소를 어디에서 알 수 있어(요)?

yeo-gi ju-so-reul eo-di-e-seo al ssu i-sseo(-yo)?

Missing Children

My daughter is missing.

내 딸을 잃어버렸어요.

nae dda-reul i-reo-beo-ryeo-sseo-yo

Where did you lose her?

따님을 어디에서 잃어버렸나요?

dda-ni-meul eo-di-e-seo i-reo-beo-ryeon-na-yo?

What does your son look like?

아드님이 어떻게 생겼어요?

a-deu-ni-mi eo-ddeo-ke saeng-gyeo-sseo-yo?

아드님의 인상착의를 말씀해 주세요.

a-deu-ni-me in-sang-cha-gi-reul mal-sseum-hae ju-se-yo

Could you make an announcement for a missing child?

미아 방송을 해 주시겠어요?

mi-a bang-song-eul hae ju-si-ge-sseo-yo?

Where's the home for missing children?

미아보호소가 어디예요?

mi-a-bo-ho-so-ga eo-di-ye-yo?

I want to report a missing child.

미아 신고를 하려고요.

mi-a sin-go-reul ha-ryeo-go-yo

Losing Items

Didn't you see a cell phone here?

여기에서 휴대폰 못 봤어(요)?

yeo-gi-e-seo hyu-dae-pon mot bwa-sseo(-yo)?

I can't find my keys.

내 열쇠를 찾을 수 없어(요).

nae yeol-soe-reul cha-jeul ssu eop-sseo(-yo)

I lost my bag.

가방을 잃어버렸습니다.

ga-bang-eul i-reo-beo-ryeot-sseum-ni-da

I left my purse in a taxi.

택시 안에 지갑을 두고 내렸어(요).

taek-ssi a-ne ji-ga-beul du-go nae-ryeo-sseo(-yo)

I don't remember where I lost it.

어디에서 잃어버렸는지 생각나지 않아(요).

eo-di-e-seo i-reo-beo-ryeon-neun-ji saeng-gak-na-ji a-na(-yo)

You'd better hurry and report the card missing.

빨리 카드 분실 신고를 하세요.

bbal-ri ka-deu bun-sil sin-go-reul ha-se-yo

Lost & Found

Where is the Lost and Found?

분실물 보관소가 어디예요?

bun-sil-mul bo-gwan-so-ga eo-di-ye-yo?

Fill out this lost baggage form.

분실물 신청서를 작성해 주세요.

bun-sil-mul sin-cheong-seo-reul jak-sseong-hae ju-se-yo

I'm here to pick up my baggage that I lost.

분실한 짐을 찾으러 왔습니다.

bun-sil-han ji-meul cha-jeu-reo wat-sseum-ni-da

The Lost and Found office is right over there.

분실물 보관소는 바로 저기에 있어(요).

bun-sil-mul bo-gwan-so-neun ba-ro jeo-gi-e i-sseo(-yo)

You'll have to check with the Lost and Found.

분실물 보관소에 가서 확인해 봐(요).

bun-sil-mul bo-gwan-so-e ga-seo hwa-gin-hae bwa(-yo)

Robbery

\# Robber! / Thief!

도둑이야!

do-du-gi-ya!

\# My wallet was stolen.

내 지갑을 도둑 맞았어(요).

nae ji-ga-beul do-duk ma-ja-sseo(-yo)

\# He stole my purse.

그는 내 지갑을 훔쳤어(요).

geu-neun nae ji-ga-beul hum-cheo-sseo(-yo)

\# Someone took my bag.

누가 내 가방을 가져갔어(요).

nu-ga nae ga-bang-eul ga-jeo-ga-sseo(-yo)

\# I'd like to report a robbery.

도둑을 신고하고 싶어(요).

do-du-geul sin-go-ha-go si-peo(-yo)

369

Recently there have been break-ins in the neighborhood.

최근 이웃에 도둑이 들었어(요).

choe-qeun i-u-se do-du-gi deu-reo-sseo(-yo)

It looks like we were robbed.

도둑맞은 거 같아(요).

do-dung-ma-jeun geo ga-ta(-yo)

My house was burglarized when I was away only briefly.

잠시 집을 비운 사이 도둑이 들었어(요).

jam-si ji-beul bi-un sa-i do-du-gi deu-reo-sseo(-yo)

My house was robbed last night.

어젯밤에 우리 집에 도둑이 들었어(요).

eo-jet-bba-me u-ri ji-be do-du-gi deu-reo-sseo(-yo)

My bike was stolen last night.

지난밤에 내 자전거를 도난당했어(요).

ji-nan-ba-me nae ja-jeon-geo-reul do-nan-dang-hae-sseo(-yo)

That's a burglar alarm.

그것은 도난방지 시스템이에요.

geu-geo-seun do-nan-bang-ji si-seu-te-mi-e-yo

Pickpockets

Catch the pickpocket!

소매치기 잡아라!

so-mae-chi-gi ja-ba-ra!

I've been pickpocketed.

소매치기 당했어(요).

so-mae-chi-gi dang-hae-sseo(-yo)

Beware of pickpockets!

소매치기를 조심하세요!

so-mae-chi-gi-reul jo-sim-ha-se-yo!

Passengers, keep an eye on your belongings so that no one snatches them.

승객 여러분, 소매치기를 당하지 않도록 소지품에 주의하십시오.

seung-gaek yeo-reo-bun, so-mae-chi-gi-reul dang-ha-ji an-to-rok so-ji-pu-me ju-i-ha-sip-ssi-o

A pickpoket got his hand into my bag.

소매치기가 내 가방에 손을 넣었어(요).

so-mae-chi-gi-ga nae ga-bang-e so-neul neo-eo-sseo(-yo)

Fraud

I was scammed.

사기를 당했어(요).

sa-gi-reul dang-hae-sseo(-yo)

He is a con artist.

그는 사기꾼이에요.

geu-neun sa-gi-ggu-ni-e-yo

Don't take me for a ride!

사기치지 마!

sa-gi-chi-ji ma!

It's obviously a scam.

그건 순전히 사기예요.

geu-geon sun-jeon-hi sa-gi-ye-yo

He bilked me of ten million won last month.

그는 지난달에 천만 원을 사기 쳤어(요).

geu-neun ji-nan-da-re cheon-man wo-neul sa-gi
cheo-sseo(-yo)

His promise was a big lie.

그의 약속은 순 사기였어(요).

geu-e yak-sso-geun sun sa-gi-yeo-sseo(-yo)

That's white-collar crime.

그건 화이트칼라 범죄예요.

geu-geon hwa-i-teu-kal-ra beom-joe-ye-yo

He conned me out of 2 million won.

그는 내게 사기를 쳐서 2백만 원을
빼앗았어(요).

geu-neun nae ge sa-gi-reul cheo-seo i-baeng-man wo-neul
bbae-a-sa-sseo(-yo)

He was arrested on a charge of fraud.

그는 사기죄로 체포됐어(요).

geu-neun sa-gi-joe-ro che-po-dwae-sseo(-yo)

I got ripped off by a taxi driver.

택시 기사한테 사기당했어(요).

taek-ssi gi-sa-han-te sa-gi-dang-hae-sseo(-yo)

I believed the con artist's story hook, line
and sinker.

그 사기꾼의 말을 다 믿었어(요).

geu sa-gi-ggu-ne ma-reul da mi-deo-sseo(-yo)

He is a crook inside and out.

그는 완전히 사기꾼이에요.

geu-neun wan-jeon-hi sa-gi-ggu-ni-e-yo

Don't believe everyone you meet.

만나는 모든 사람을 믿지 마(세요).

man-na-neun mo-deun sa-ra-meul mit-jji ma(-se-yo)

Police Reports

Where is the nearest police station?

여기에서 가장 가까운 경찰서가 어디예요?

yeo-gi-e-seo ga-jang ga-gga-un gyeong-chal-sseo-ga
eo-di-ye-yo?

Report it to the police.

경찰에 신고해라.

gyeong-cha-re sin-go-hae-ra

I called the police right away.

즉시 경찰에 신고했어(요).

jeuk-ssi gyeong-cha-re sin-go-hae-sseo(-yo)

You'd better come down to the station and report it.

경찰서에 가서 신고하는 게 좋겠어(요).

gyeong chal-sseo-e ga-seo sin-go-ha-neun ge
jo-ke-sseo(-yo)

Why didn't you report it to the police?

왜 경찰에 신고하지 않았어(요)?

wae gyeong-cha-re sin-go-ha-ji a-na-sseo(-yo)?

Such cases must be notified to the police.

이런 사건들은 경찰에 알려야 해(요).

i-reon sa-ggeon-deu-reun gyeong-cha-re al-ryeo-ya hae(-yo)

Car Accidents

I had a car accident.

교통사고를 당했어(요).

gyo-tong-sa-go-reul dang-hae-sseo(-yo)

I witnessed a traffic accident.

교통사고를 목격했어(요).

gyo-tong-sa-go-reul mok-ggyeo-kae-sseo(-yo)

She hit me from behind.

그녀가 뒤에서 박았어(요).

geu-nyeo-ga dwi-e-seo ba-ga-sseo(-yo)

When did the traffic accident happen?

그 교통사고는 언제 일어났어(요)?

geu gyo-tong-sa-go-neun eon-je i-reo-na-sseo(-yo)?

This is an accident black spot.

이곳은 교통사고 다발지점이에요.

i-go-seun gyo-tong-sa-go da-bal-ji-jeo-mi-e-yo

Always get their name, license number and insurance information.

항상 상대방의 이름, 면허 번호와 보험 정보를 받아야 해(요).

hang-sang sang-dae-bang-e i-reum, myeon-heo beon-ho-wa bo-heom jeong-bo-reul ba-da-ya hae(-yo)

Accidents

\# The boy fell into the water and drowned.

소년은 물에 빠져서 익사했어(요).

so-nyeo-neun mu-re bba-jeo-seo ik-ssa-hae-sseo(-yo)

\# I heard that you had a skateboard accident last week.

지난주에 스케이트보드 타다가 사고 났다면서(요).

ji-nan-ju-e seu-ke-i-teu-bo-deu ta-da-ga sa-go nat-dda-myeon-seo(-yo)

\# He got almost killed by an electric shock.

그는 감전되어 죽을 뻔했어(요).

geu-neun gam-jeon-doe-eo ju-geul bbeon-hae-sseo(-yo)

\# My son is unconscious after falling down the stairs.

우리 아들은 계단에서 떨어져 의식 불명이에요.

u-ri a-deu-reun gye-da-ne-seo ddeo-reo-jeo ui-sik bul-myeong-i-e-yo

This morning I slipped on the ice.

오늘 아침 빙판에서 미끄러졌어(요).

o-neul a-chim bing-pa-ne-seo mi-ggeu-reo-jeo-sseo(-yo)

I tripped over a rock.

돌에 걸려 넘어졌어(요).

do-re geol-ryeo neo-meo-jeo-sseo(-yo)

I tripped on the stairs and nearly broke my neck.

계단을 헛디뎌서 목을 다칠 뻔했어(요).

gye-da-neul heot-ddi-dyeo-seo mo-geul da-chil bbeon-hae-sseo(-yo)

I fell off my bicycle.

자전거를 타다가 넘어졌어(요).

ja-jeon-geo-reul ta-da-ga neo-meo-jeo-sseo(-yo)

My grandma fell and banged her knees.

할머니가 넘어지셔서 무릎을 다치셨어(요).

hal-meo-ni-ga neo-meo-ji-syeo-seo mu-reu-peul da-chi-syeo-sseo(-yo)

Seung-woo lost the use of his left leg because of the accident.
승우는 사고로 왼쪽 다리를 쓰지 못해(요).
seung u neun sa go ro oen jjok da ri reul sseu ji mo tae(yo)

Fire

Fire!
불이야!
bu-ri-ya!

Call 119!
어서 119에 전화해(요)!
eo-seo il-ril-gu-e jeon-hwa-hae(-yo)!

A fire accident happened last night.
어젯밤에 화재가 발생했어(요).
eo-jet-ba-me hwa-jae-ga bal-ssaeng-hae-sseo(-yo)

Last night a fire destroyed this building.
이 건물은 어젯밤 화재로 불타버렸어(요).
i geon-mu-reun eo-jet-bbam hwa-jae-ro
bul-ta-beo-ryeo-sseo(-yo)

The people escaped from the town because of the fire.

화재가 발생하여, 사람들이 대피했어(요).

hwa-jae-ga bal-ssaeng-ha-yeo, sa-ram-deu-ri
dae-pi-hae-sseo(-yo)

Careless is often cause of the fires.

부주의해서 화재가 자주 발생하죠.

bu-ju-i-hae-seo hwa-jae-ga ja-ju bal-ssaeng-ha-jyo

That's a fire truck. Can you hear the siren?

소방차예요. 사이렌 소리 들려요?

so-bang-cha-ye-yo. sa-i-ren so-ri deul-ryeo-yo?

The firemen got to the fire in 5 minutes.

소방관들은 5분 만에 화재 현장에
도착했어(요).

so-bang-gwan-deu-reun o-bun ma-ne hwa-jae hyeon-jang-e
do-cha-kae-sseo(-yo)

What caused the fire?

그 화재 원인은 뭐예요?

geu hwa-jae wo-ni-neun mwo-ye-yo?

Smoke from the fire accident burned my throat and eyes.

화재에서 발생한 연기 때문에 목과 눈이 화끈거렸어(요).

hwa-jae-e-seo bal-ssaeng-han yeon-gi ddae-mu-ne mok-ggwa nu-ni hwa-ggeun-geo-ryeo-sseo(-yo)

If the fire alarm goes on, it's only a test.

화재경보가 울리면, 그냥 테스트예요.

hwa-jae-gyeong-bo-ga ul-ri-myeon, geu-nyang te-seu-teu-ye-yo

Earthquakes

Did you feel that earthquake last night?

간밤에 지진 느꼈어(요)?

gan-ba-me ji-jin neu-ggyeo-sseo(-yo)?

How much damage did the earthquake do?

지진으로 얼마나 타격을 입었어(요)?

ji-ji-neu-ro eol-ma-na ta-gyeo-geul i-beo-sseo(-yo)?

The village was destroyed by an earthquake.

저 마을은 지진으로 파괴됐어(요).

jeo ma-eu-reun ji-ji-neu-ro pa-goe-dwae-sseo(-yo)

A 8.2 magnitude earthquake hit the region.

그 지역에 진도 8.2의 지진이 발생했어(요).

geu ji-yeo-ge jin-do pal-jjeo-mi-e ji-ji-ni
bal-ssaeng-hae-sseo(-yo)

What did you do when the earthquake hit the building?

지진이 일어났을 때 건물에서 어떻게 했어(요)?

ji-ji-ni i-reo-na-sseul ddae geon-mu-re-seo eo-ddeo-ke hae-sseo(-yo)?

The earthquake caused a lot of damage on the plants.

지진으로 농작물이 많이 훼손됐어(요).

ji-ji-neu-ro nong-jang-mu-ri ma-ni hwe-son-dwae-sseo(-yo)

Were there any aftershocks?

여진이 있었어(요)?

yeo-ji-ni i-sseo-sseo(-yo)?

This building will not be broken when the earthquake hits.

이 건물은 지진이 일어나도 괜찮아(요).

i geon-mu-reun ji-ji-ni i-reo-na-do gwaen-cha-na(-yo)

The entire house shook when the earthquake occurred.

지진이 발생하자, 집 전체가 흔들거렸어(요).

ji-ji-ni bal-ssaeng-ha-ja, jip jeon-che-ga
heun-deul-geo-ryeo-sseo(-yo)

Are earthquakes common around here?

이 근처에 지진이 흔해(요)?

i geun-cheo-e ji-ji-ni heun-hae(-yo)?